Where the Wild Strawberries Grow

DAVID & CLAUDIA ARP

CHARIOT
VICTOR
PUBLISHING

A DIVISION OF COOK COMMUNICATIONS

Chariot • Victor Publishing
Cook Communications, Colorado Springs, CO 80918
Cook Communications, Paris, Ontario
Kingsway Communications, Eastbourne, England

WHERE THE WILD STRAWBERRIES GROW
© 1996 by David and Claudia Arp

All Scripture quotations in this publication, unless otherwise noted, are from the *Holy Bible, New International Version.* Copyright ® 1973, 1978, 1984, International Bible Society.

All Scripture quotations labeled NASB are from the *New American Standard Bible,* ® the Lockman Foundation 1960, 1962, 1963, 1968, 1971, 1972, 1973, 1975, 1977.

Cover design by Steve Diggs and Friends
Cover illustration by Steve Diggs and Friends
First printing, 1996
Printed in the United States of America
00 99 98 97 96   5 4 3 2 1

Published in association with the literary agency of Alive Communications, Inc.
1465 Kelly Johnson Blvd., Suite 320, Colorado Springs, Colorado 80920

Library of Congress Cataloging-in-Publication Data

Arp, Dave.
        Where the wild strawberries grow/ by David and Claudia Arp.
        p.   cm.
        ISBN 0-7814-0291-3
        1. Marriage.   2. Marriage--Religious aspects--Christianity.
    I. Arp, Claudia. II. Title.
    HQ734.A694 1996
    248.8'44--dc20   96-5115
                                                                      CIP

Contents

Chapter 1

Where the Wild Strawberries Grow

When spring arrives, so does yard work—not our favorite activity. So at breakfast one lovely spring Saturday, Dave announced he was going to "do the yard." Claudia was delighted. To say that Dave doesn't enjoy yard work is an understatement. So all day, Claudia stayed out of his way—she didn't want to sidetrack the gardener.

Late that afternoon, Dave resurfaced—dirty, tired, sore muscles and all—but he had "done the yard" and wanted to show off his accomplishments. So together we went outside to take a tour.

Everything looked transformed—the lawn was neatly manicured, the shrubs were trimmed, and the weeds were history! Claudia was thrilled until we came to her strawberry patch. All of her prized strawberry plants were gone. All that remained were the unwanted, useless wild strawberries.

"You ruined my strawberries!" she exclaimed. "How could you do that after all the hours I've worked to cultivate them? I can't believe you didn't at least ask what to pull!" Claudia's anger made Dave wish he had covered the whole yard with concrete.

Do you ever honestly try to help your marriage team, but make a mess instead? You get irritated with each other and say things you later regret. At times like these, you need to clear the air and forgive one another.

Claudia tried to do just that. "Dave," she said, "I didn't mean to attack you. I know you didn't intentionally kill my strawberries. I'm just so frustrated and disappointed my strawberry plants are gone. This was the year we were going to have strawberries on ice cream, strawberries on cereal, and strawberries on shortcake!"

Dave responded, "I'm frustrated, too. I spent the whole day in the yard, my body hurts, I'm tired, and now I find out I did it wrong. It's just that the wild strawberries actually had little red berries on them. I assumed they were the good strawberries! I didn't mean to ruin your strawberries. I'm sorry."

About that time we eyed the strawberry victims. The cultured plants were in a heap in the driveway. As we calmed down, we came up with a plan. First, we pulled the wild strawberries. Then we replanted the real ones. Before sunset the strawberries and our relationship were restored. We were back on the same team.

Our story is about more than a strawberry patch. The wild strawberries are like the unwanted weeds in our marriage garden. Sometimes the young, good strawberries are mistakenly uprooted while the wild, worthless strawberries are left to grow and flourish. Check your own marriage patch for what really needs to be uprooted:

- Have I planted any unkind words?
- Have I broken my mate's trust?
- Have I selfishly demanded my own rights?
- Have I overcommitted myself again?

Many times we have the best of intentions, but still uproot the wrong things. Can you identify with the mate who:

- Mailed the tax forms to the IRS, but forgot to send the check?
- Didn't notice a bright red baby bib sneaking into the

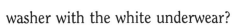

washer with the white underwear?

- Ran out to get baby food, but in haste got "chunky" instead of "strained"?

The good strawberries represent the positive things we do to nurture our friendship with our spouses—simple kindnesses and considerations, such as:

- Washing the dishes when it's not your turn.
- Getting up at 2:00 A.M. for the potty run.
- Using the words *thank you*, *please*, *I'm sorry*, and *I forgive you.*

Cultivating a relationship in the closeness of marriage must include forgiveness. No two people agree on everything, so we have a lot of opportunities to forgive and ask for forgiveness. Maybe you're in that situation right now. If so, here are some suggestions:

- Keep short accounts. Don't let small irritations grow into big ones.
- Ask for forgiveness today. There's wisdom in the words, "Don't let the sun go down on your anger."
- Share how you feel. Let statements reflect back on you. You could say something like, "I'm sorry I shouted at you. I felt angry and frustrated. Will you forgive me?"
- Forgive your mate when he/she blows it.

Forgiveness is to a marriage what tilling is to a garden. It softens the hard soil of friction that occurs in the closeness of daily marriage challenges. Ephesians 4:32 tells us to be kind and compassionate, forgiving each other. Our example? God's forgiveness through Christ.

As we think back to our strawberry patch, we're glad we were willing to forgive each other. After all, our marriage is more important than strawberries. By the way, the replanted strawberry plants lived, thrived, and that year we did have fresh strawberries on ice cream, on cereal, and on homemade shortcake. The next year, Dave pruned the blackberries—but that's a story for another time!

Chapter 2

The Making of a Healthy Marriage

At a recent neighborhood party, a young mother asked in frustration, "Can anybody tell me what a healthy marriage looks like? I want to build our marriage, but life is so hectic with three preschoolers, there isn't time. Besides, I don't know where to start."

Others shared their feelings and a lively discussion followed as we talked about characteristics of a healthy marriage. At the top of our list were commitment, vital faith in God, and good communication. Others mentioned romance, being on the same team, and having common goals. But if we had to put it in a nutshell, we'd say, "A healthy marriage is one in which there is a willingness to find time to work on the marriage relationship."

Another parent asked, "Can you really work on your marriage and your family at the same time? There are only so many hours in the day and my teenagers are energy zappers!"

Our answer? An emphatic yes! We're convinced that the best backdrop for building a strong, healthy, and growing family is to have a strong, healthy, and growing marriage. The two go hand in hand and you must find time for both!

According to a poll of twelve thousand people, the number-one cause of marriage breakups is the failure of partners to work at their marriage! No one plans to be a divorce statistic, but in today's fast-paced world with added pressures of parenting, it's easy to let the marriage relationship slip. Think about it—the number-one cause of divorce is preventable! You can do something to ensure that you are not a statistic!

We took our own informal survey and asked people, "What is the top reason couples don't work on their marriages?" The overwhelming answer was, "lack of time."

It takes a lot of time to grow a healthy marriage. We learned this the hard way. We've been working on our marriage for more than thirty-three years. Before we had children, it was easier to find time for each other; but after having three boys in five years, we were slowly becoming strangers.

We kept looking for a large block of time to clean the barnacles off our marriage ship, but you know the story: "We'll talk about that tomorrow. Next month. Next summer. Next year!" It didn't happen—until we moved to Europe. Part of our culture shock was getting used to being with each other. Suddenly, we found the time we needed to work on our relationship. Even then, it wasn't easy—especially with three young children who had their own needs. But gradually we began to chip away at those barnacles and our marriage began to grow.

You may be thinking, "If we could move to the other side of the world and get away from all our responsibilities and the pressures of parenting, we could work on our marriage, too!" We've discovered that you don't have to have large blocks of time to work on your marriage. You do need some time, however, and you can find it in little places. Try these two tips:

- Take time to talk. Start by carving out some time. Looking at your schedule and family situation, identify little bits of time you can call your own. One couple with teenagers has a standing breakfast date each Saturday morning. They're

back home before their kids even wake
up. Another couple gets up fifteen minutes earlier to
talk about their day, read the Bible, and pray together.
(We tried this at our house and it didn't work. Our kids
had a motion sensor that said, "Get up! Mom and Dad are
up early!")

- Have some fun. Once you claim your own time, make a list
  of fun things you would like to do together. Then choose
  one and do it! Take the initiative. Go ahead and get the sitter—it's worth the hassle.

Whether you have toddlers, teens, or children somewhere in
between, or even if you are in the empty nest, start today and
use the time you have to build your marriage.

Chapter 3

A Verse for All Seasons

Like a lot of their friends, we thought Carl and Sally had a great marriage. They were key leaders in their church. They appeared to have a deep, abiding faith. Carl spent his free time coaching the youth soccer league. Sally ran the women's ministry. So when Carl packed up and left without a word of explanation, we were among the many who were shocked.

You don't have to look far to see Christian marriages breaking up. Sadly, this includes Christian leaders and pastors. In some circles, the rate of divorce seems to be at epidemic proportions. One pastor recently told us that he spends most of his time counseling couples and trying to help them keep their marriages intact.

Why are Christians divorcing in record numbers? Unfortunately, being a Christian doesn't guarantee marital success. The Bible's principles for building positive relationships work, but only if you know them and apply them. Though Carl and Sally loved God and were trying to serve Him, they were not applying biblical principles in their marriage. They didn't have a "Christian" marriage.

What makes a marriage uniquely Christian? When asked what was the greatest commandment of all, Jesus replied, "Love the Lord your God with all your heart and with all your soul and with all your mind and with all your strength. . . . 'Love your

neighbor as yourself.' There is no commandment greater than these" (Mark 12:30,31).

In the New Testament, *neighbor* means the person closest to
you. For any married person, that is your marriage partner, the
one you've chosen to share life with at its deepest and most intimate level. If you love your spouse as you love yourself, you'll
have his or her best interests at heart. You'll want to serve, not
be served. You'll resist the urge to manipulate or pull power
plays. You'll do your best to have a relationship based on love
and trust. These basic principles will put you well on your way
to having a Christian marriage.

Not only did Jesus have much to say about building positive
relationships, but He also modeled those principles. His life on
Earth demonstrated love in action. So many times our marital
conflicts could be resolved if we followed the example of Christ.
Too often we are "me-centered" and want things to work out
"my" way. Christ taught just the opposite approach.

Does Christ make a difference in your marriage? In *The
Sacred Fire*, David and Vera Mace write: "What the New
Testament makes possible for a man, a woman, or a married
couple is an encounter with Jesus of Nazareth. Therefore, it is
only those who have encountered the ever-living Christ and
have surrendered their lives to Him who will surely know how
to make their marriages truly Christian."

Christ demonstrated how to live, and He will empower us to
express love, to be sensitive to the needs of others, to be open
and honest, to act considerately and unselfishly, to deal with
anger and conflict, to forgive and be reconciled, and to reflect
His love in our love for one another. Then our marriages will be
truly Christian.

A Christian marriage involves three—the husband, the wife,

and God. Picture a triangle with God at the top, you on one side, and your mate on the other side. As you grow closer to God, you will move closer to each other. Our Christian faith gives us a common focus in life. It's simply foundational to our having an enriched, healthy Christian marriage. Our faith in God has much to do with our commitment to growth and permanence in our marriage. What is the foundation for your marriage? Are you basing your marriage on biblical principles? Is Christ empowering you? Are you following His model and teachings?

A number of years ago, a pastor encouraged us to search the Scriptures to find a passage that we could claim for our marriage. We encourage you to do the same. Our special marriage passage is Ecclesiastes 4:9-12. These verses describe what we want for our marriage relationship:

"Two are better than one, because they have a good return for their work: If one falls down, his friend can help him up. But pity the man who falls and has no one to help him up! Also, if two lie down together, they will keep warm. But how can one keep warm alone? Though one may be overpowered, two can defend themselves. A cord of three strands is not quickly broken."

What a beautiful picture of marriage! It's certainly not a picture of a perfect relationship. Both fall down from time to time. But even then, the third strand holds the marriage together. The third strand that holds us when we fall is God, the Holy Spirit.

What describes your marriage? What would you like to describe it? We challenge you to search Scripture and choose your own verse. As Christians, the Bible is our resource to make a good marriage better—to make our marriages go the distance.

Chapter 4

Detour Ahead!

City traffic drives us crazy. Recently we found ourselves in the middle of six lanes of madness! The cars weaving in and out of lanes reminded us of an arcade video game.

When children come along and careers take off, the roads of our lives widen. How many lanes do you feel like you are trying to monitor?

We have at least eight. We're partners in marriage, parents, grandparents, peers of our friends, professionals in our work, relatives of extended families, members of our church, and members of the body of Christ. No wonder we zip right by the "rest areas" of life and may even be in the wrong lane when it's time to take an exit. How can a couple avoid road hazards and superhighway fast-lane stress?

Observe the Road Signs

Signs tell us where to turn and keep us from getting lost. They let us know how fast to go and warn us of impending dangers. Here are some signs that it's time to drive in the slow lane for a while:

- You have a list of topics to discuss with your spouse, but no time to discuss them.
- You're going to bed later and getting up more tired. When you do get to bed, your mind keeps racing—you need to

balance the checkbook, pick up the clothes that have been at the cleaners for a month, and make dental appointments for everyone.

- You're more irritable and grouchy. Today you lost your cool while trying to help your four year old memorize, "Love is patient and kind!"
- You make excuses about why you're too busy: "Things will slow down after basketball season ends. When Billy sleeps through the night and Jennifer is potty trained, life will be simpler."

Learn to Drive Defensively

Watch out for other crazy drivers—the ones who sideswipe you by pressing you into commitments you can't keep. This may not be the best time to help remodel your in-laws' kitchen or to take on a volunteer job. Watch out for the pothole of over-commitment. Learn to say no.

Lift Your Foot off the Gas

You don't have to race at breakneck speeds just because everyone else is. If you need to slow down, make a list of things you can delay doing. For example, if you have a new baby, face it, things are going to be crazy—at least for a couple of months. Remember, life comes in seasons. When you're parenting small children, your options are limited. Learn to pace yourself.

When the traffic seems extremely hectic, try these suggestions:

- Splurge and use paper plates and cups for twenty-four hours. (Eat finger foods, and you won't even have to wash silverware!)
- When you're too tired to clean, close doors.

- Prepare a bubble bath for your tired mate.
- After the kids are in bed, meet your mate in the living room for low-fat frozen yogurt and conversation.
- Sneak times to pray together.
- Schedule one afternoon a month to be all alone. Take a walk, get some extra rest, or do whatever you want to do.
- Daydream. Borrowed books and magazines make finding ideas easy. Have fun talking with your spouse about all the possibilities.
- Consider throwing out (or selling) the TV so that you will be forced to do other things together. If you can't go cold turkey, give up cable, or hide the set in the closet for a few weeks.
- Play board games together.
- Have a grocery store date. It can be fairly pleasant without children along.
- One couple told us: "We go shopping for something with no intention of buying—cars, motor homes, anything. We act crazy and lap up the sales people's attention. Like the Cat in the Hat says, 'It's fun to have fun, but you have to know how.'"

Work together with your mate to overcome fast-lane stress. You may even have a little fun in the process!

Chapter 5

Something to Sleep On

Jet lag is first cousin to insomnia. Just home from Hong Kong, we were trying to adjust to the thirteen-hour time difference and found it difficult to sleep.

Few things are more irritating than insomnia. Neither of us likes it, but we each handle it in different ways. When Dave can't sleep, he simply gets up and plays with his computer. Claudia uses the time to worry about all the things that overwhelm her.

What wakes you up in the middle of the night? Is it the awesome responsibility of parenting? Uncertainty about your job? Fear that your marriage could somehow become a horrible statistic? While we know Scripture tells us to cast all our cares on the Lord, it isn't easy—especially in the middle of the night!

With our bodies still on Hong Kong time, it was easy to get up for early church. Afterward, over a late breakfast, we talked about our situation. It wasn't just not being able to sleep, we felt overwhelmed with life. We're great list makers. Writing down everything we needed to do helped. But what helped even more was to commit to the Lord our cares, concerns, and sleeplessness.

Prayer Obstacles

A unique resource we have in a Christian marriage is prayer. God delights in the praise and prayers of His people. He reminds us that if we lack wisdom, we can simply ask and He will give it liberally (James 1:5). As parents and partners, we desperately need it, but why is it so hard to pray together? We can think of at least three obstacles:

1. **My mate is uninterested or is not a Christian**. Maybe your mate has no interest in praying with you, or isn't a Christian. We were at that point in the early years of our marriage. Our advice? Hang in there, and in the meantime, pray for your mate. But watch what you pray! Claudia remembers praying that Dave would get excited about his faith. When God answered, she was thrilled until Dave decided to quit his secure job and go into full-time Christian work!

2. **We're not on the same track**. When a relationship isn't running smoothly, it's difficult, if not impossible, to pray together. Sometimes the only thing you can pray is, "Lord, help us get back on track so we can pray together!" If you feel so far apart that you can't even do that, pray alone that the Lord will restore your relationship.

3. **My spouse is a prayer hog**. Sometimes during prayer times together, Claudia would cover all the bases before Dave even prayed. All that was left for him to say was "Amen." We learned to make a prayer list first, then took turns praying through our list. What goes on the list? Anything that concerns you. Maybe you're struggling with priorities, time pressures, your budget, or dealing with a strong-willed child or wayward teenager.

A word of caution: Don't use prayer to attack your mate like the pair who prayed, "Lord, please help Charlie understand me and stop criticizing me in front of the children," and "Make Gladys more sensitive to my needs and to be a more responsive lover." If you're just beginning to pray together, don't start with the most tense situation.

How to Have a Prayer Date

Setting aside time to pray together brings us closer together. Our prayer dates are not very structured, but here are some of the things we do:

- Read the Scriptures together.
- Talk about answered prayers and how God has led us in the past.
- Write down specific prayer requests.
- Make a list of things we want to pray about for each family member. (We make duplicates to tuck in our Bibles.)
- And most important, we actually pray together!

Why not take the time right now to plan your own prayer date? Believe us, it works. We still deal with jet lag-induced insomnia, but even that is getting better. Now in the middle of the night, as Dave sits at his computer, he enters items for our next prayer date. And being the considerate husband that he is, he put a pad and pencil on the bedside table for Claudia to record her middle-of-the-night worries. The next morning we combine lists, so when it's time for our next prayer date, we're ready.

Chapter 6

The Marriage Diet

Our secret is out! Someone actually spotted our grocery cart. "I see," our friend commented, stopping us during an emergency grocery run, "you're going to be eating easy, lite, and low-fat."

Recently, life for us has been anything but "easy, lite, and low-fat." You can probably identify. In the midst of family life, how do you find time to build your marriage? Sometimes you just have to grab it. Before our emergency grocery store run, we did just that.

We had spent the previous three days at a beautiful retreat center perched by the side of a lake in the North Georgia mountains. Walking paths abounded and the flowers and foliage begged us to come outside and enjoy them. A pet deer named "Precious" waited at the door to accompany us on a walk. The conference's sessions, however, started early in the morning and went nonstop until late in the evening, with few free moments. The last session adjourned late, and we were already behind schedule. As we packed our car, Claudia lamented, "It's a shame to be around such beauty and not get to enjoy it."

Dave replied, "What's the big hurry? Let's walk around the lake before we head home."

That's just what we did. For us, the following thirty minutes were the highlight of the whole conference. We regrouped and reconnected with each other. We talked about what we had gained during the past three days and how our new insights would help us relate better to each other and to other families.

But it would have been so easy to jump in our car, race off, and miss a pleasant and significant interlude.

What about you? Are you missing pleasant interludes as you rush through the years? Are you taking time to enjoy the flowers, to notice butterflies, and to pet the tame deer? What can you do to grab time for two in your busy world?

On your next trip to the grocery store, take a practical step toward enriching your relationship with your mate, especially if you're feeling like life is more hectic than it has ever been. Use the words *easy*, *lite* and *low-fat* to come up with how you and your spouse can grab time together. Here are some suggestions:

Easy
- Make a phone call or write a letter to your mate to say, "I love you and I'm thinking about you."
- Give your mate an extra hug and kiss tonight.

Lite
- Slip out together for frozen yogurt.
- After the children are in bed, pull out the good china and linens, blow the dust off the dining-room chairs, and enjoy a mellow salad dinner by candlelight.
- Picnic in the back yard with vegetables and "lite" dip.

Low-fat
- 2% Marriage Enrichment Time: That's twenty-nine minutes a day in a twenty-four-hour day. Set aside your 2% and claim it.
- 1% Marriage Enrichment Time: If life is really wild, 1% will make a difference. That's just fourteen minutes a day.

• Ride bikes, jog, or take a walk together.

Each time you race through the grocery store, choose one thing you're going to do that day to build your relationship with your mate. Psalm 90:12 says, "Teach us to number our days aright, that we may gain a heart of wisdom." Take that a step further, and number your hours and minutes.

Remember, your children will wait while you grab your minutes together. But your marriage relationship will not wait until your children grow up. Now is the time to build your marriage!

Chapter 7

What's Your
Marriage Potential?

We'll never forget the first time we met David and Vera
Mace. For years we'd studied their books and had been greatly
influenced by their writings. Now we had the opportunity to
attend a training conference at Black Mountain, North Carolina,
led by the Maces. It was a small group, so we all had the opportunity to chat with David and Vera.

We were immediately impressed with their low-key,
approachable natures. We soon discovered that they had been
married for almost fifty years, yet their relationship was so alive,
vibrant, and contagious! They lived and modeled what they
taught, and it was so refreshing!

Just being around them encouraged us to renew and re-
evaluate our own marriage. The Maces challenged us to take a
Marriage Potential Inventory.* This exercise has been success-
fully used to help couples discuss their expectations and assess
their relationships. It showed us that our marriage still had
much potential yet to be developed.

This inventory can do the same thing for you! Take a few
minutes to rate your marriage on a scale of one to ten in each of
the following areas—ten represents a very high level of satisfaction, and one represents low satisfaction. Do this separately,
then come together and talk with your partner about your
ratings.

Marriage Potential Inventory

- Common goals and values
- Commitment to growth
- Communication skills
- Creative use of conflict
- Appreciation or affection
- Agreement on gender roles
- Cooperation and teamwork
- Sexual fulfillment
- Money management
- Decision-making

"The purpose of the exercise," the Maces told us, "is to encourage honest appraisal, promote dialogue, and help you plan for growth in your marriage." They explained that if one partner scores lower than the other in one area, it may mean that person has higher expectations in that area. If there are significant differences in scoring, it may mean one of two things: differences in expectations, or differences in your assessment of how you're performing as a couple. Either way, the inventory is a great tool to talk about your expectations and to realize how much potential for growth your marriage has.

Over the years we have tuned-up our marriage using the Marriage Potential Inventory. When our scores are widely different, it's a clear sign that we at least need to talk. Usually, it also indicates that we need to do some work.

Perhaps you have different expectations in the area of money management. One of you grew up in a home where money was abundant, while the other has been a penny-pincher since age three. Here's an opportunity to talk it out and adopt a united strategy.

We promise that no matter how you approach this exercise or use it, it will show you that your marriage has great potential!

* From David and Vera Mace, *A.C.M.E. Newsletter*, Vol. 16, No. 4, April 1988.

Chapter 8

The Dance of the Fingers

Some of the things that cause tension in a marriage aren't moral issues. They aren't right or wrong—they're just irritating!

While we are quite compatible, we do have our differences, and one point of contention has to do with computers. We've been members of the computer age for more than ten years. Frankly, today we'd have a hard time getting along without our trusty laptop. But it's a love-hate relationship, one mixed with irritations that occasionally raise their ugly little heads in the midst of family life.

One irritation goes all the way back to our high school days and to who took Typing I and who didn't. Claudia never won class speed races, but even in college she was familiar with the typing fundamentals. But Dave—the laid-back one, never in a hurry—took the time to write papers longhand, or he'd smile lovingly at Claudia and she would melt and volunteer to type his papers. Later, as we began to write books in the early eighties, she willingly typed the manuscripts with carbon copies.

Enter the computer age! We'll never forget our first IBM computer—it was like a tank—indestructible and reliable. We were amazed at what it would do. We quickly threw away our carbon paper and began to tickle the keys. Then the irritation manifested itself. While Claudia's typing was slow and rusty, Dave's hunt-and-peck, two-finger method drove Claudia crazy.

As the "we need to get this done fast and in the most efficient way" sort of person, she began to look for solutions. One was obvious. Dave needed to learn to type. No problem. She simply bought him a typing tutor computer program. He and our boys could all have fun learning to type! After all, shouldn't all authors be able to type?

Dave's response? While he is a fun-loving, easygoing person, he can also be a stubborn one. For the life of him, he couldn't understand what was wrong with his two-finger method. The more Claudia pushed, the more Dave resisted. We reached a complete stalemate and finally agreed to disagree. So while Claudia's fingers waltzed over the keys, Dave continued his slow two-step. The typing tutor collected dust and finally met its new owner at a garage sale. Our ultimate solution was simply to coexist, even though we danced different dances when it came to typing.

Fast-forward thirteen years. Claudia and the rest of the family are now master typists. Dave has perfected his two-finger system and might be able to win a slow race with a novice typist.

For those thirteen years we'd had a peaceful typing truce. Then we discovered e-mail. We were going to be out of the country for a couple of months and our sons convinced us to move into this twenty-first century method of communication. Wow! We tried it and discovered that it was a simple way to communicate with our family and friends. We were elated—until Claudia realized we were paying for e-mail by the minute and Dave's messages were costing more than hers because he still couldn't type! Suddenly the ghost of the "typing tutor past" resurfaced, along with Claudia's irritation. How could something resolved so many years ago resurface and again become an issue?

Isn't that so much like life?

What are the hidden irritations you need to deal with in your marriage? What about those that may not have a good solution? (Dave still hunts and pecks, and Claudia still thinks you can teach old dogs new tricks and he could learn to type if he really wanted to! In the meantime, we've learned how to compose e-mail messages off-line.)

Irritations can teach us some good principles of enriching marriages:

First, we've learned that if we don't deal with little flies in the soup, they will learn to swim and resurface. Even if there is no good solution, we need to accept each other's idiosyncrasies.

Second, we've learned that different things irritate different people. While the typing issue bugged Claudia, Claudia's refusal to learn a more updated word-processing program drove Dave crazy!

Both of us were guilty of being stubborn and unwilling to take the time to grow in our typing and computer knowledge. Likewise in our marriages, we can get so busy and caught up using our old patterns that we don't take time to grow in our relationship and in the ways we relate to each other.

The great thing about a marriage relationship is that it can always change. There is always an option to grow. Recently, Claudia took the big step to move up to a brand-new word-processing program. And yes, in a weak moment, Dave made a commitment to learn to type, but it hasn't happened yet.

Did we mention that little irritation called *procrastination*?

Chapter 9

Little Disappointments

We love bargains—especially when they're marriage builders. This one promised to make us slim, sleek, and sexy. Instead, it brought out our irritation and disappointment with each other.

We are among the myriad of people who would like to firm up and drop ten pounds, so when Claudia saw an exercise ski machine in the Saturday paper advertised for $39.99, she was sure this was the bargain for us. After all, we like to ski. Now we could have fun firming up and watching our love handles disappear. Dave, though reluctant and skeptical, was willing to placate Claudia's enthusiasm for this unbelievable bargain and said, "Sure, why don't you check it out?"

Fast-forward a couple of hours when most sane people are spending their day off pouring a second cup of coffee and taking life easy. When Claudia arrived home with the bargain bulging out of the trunk of our car, and Dave saw the huge rectangular box, he realized that someone had to put this together! The sixteen-page instruction booklet for assembling our "ski exerciser/ marriage builder" was a clue this was not going to be a fun morning. Dave has many talents, but he is not "mechanically gifted." Claudia's enthusiasm was little help.

Soon our living room resembled a bicycle repair shop. Hundreds of nuts, bolts, and parts carpeted the floor. By step eighteen, we were in deep trouble. The needed screw was missing. Our frustration and irritation levels were rising. Claudia was disappointed in Dave's lack of ingenuity, and Dave silently wished Claudia had just gone back to bed instead of bargain hunting. What had started out as a marriage builder was becoming just the opposite.

Have you ever had one of those times when a little disappointment or a frustrating experience robbed you of marital joy? The wonderful evening you planned for just the two of you is wiped out by an unexpected ear infection, or PMS clouds your usually sunny outlook on life, or your mate's little irritating habits are wearing you down.

As we lead our Marriage Alive Seminars and talk with couples around the country, we find that most marital disharmony isn't from the big disappointments in life. We usually find the grace to love each other and handle the "biggies" that come along, such as a serious illness, the sudden loss of a parent, or a traumatic job change. A special closeness comes from facing the big crises together.

Instead, it's the chronic little situations that frustrate us, such as squeezing the toothpaste the wrong way, vying for the control of the TV and VCR remotes, dealing with irritating allergies and migraine headaches, or battling the thermostat.

Whatever your little differences and irritations, how can you handle them gracefully? Is it possible to use those circumstances to draw you closer together? Yes, but at those times you need to trust each other.

To help us do this, we've agreed that when we get frustrated or disappointed with each other, we won't attack the other and we won't defend ourselves. This helps us relax and not take the situation so seriously.

We have agreed that if at all possible, we will choose to laugh rather than cry. When we don't take ourselves quite so seriously, we enjoy life more and the little things don't bother us as much—even bargains that don't work out.

The half-assembled ski exerciser on our living room floor— this was definitely a laugh or cry situation. Claudia wanted to cry, and Dave wanted to junk it and chalk up the $39.99 to experience. Neither of us wanted to spend the rest of that Saturday looking for screws.

Because of our agreement to not attack each other and to not defend ourselves, we decided to focus on the problem. Dave acknowledged that while most of Claudia's bargains are great, this one just wasn't. Together we agreed we'd had enough exercise for one day. We re-boxed our bargain, loaded it in our trunk, and took it back to the discount store. On the way home, we stopped for that second cup of coffee and decided that walking will remain our favorite marriage-builder exercise.

Walking together reminds us that marriage is a journey, not a destination. It's a marathon, not a sprint. Marriage is for the long haul, and when we give each other permission to be less than perfect, when we accept each other's shortcomings and handle the little disappointments gracefully and with humor, we just may find we are growing closer together. What a bargain— we can save our $39.99!

Chapter 10

And Baby Makes Three

What has the energy of an atomic bomb, provides more entertainment than a Broadway show, is as light as a feather, but can light up the world with her smile? Our granddaughter, Sophie!

Sophie adds sunshine to our lives. And when she was first born, she certainly brought changes for her parents. Do you remember when you transitioned from "just you and me" to "you and me—and baby makes three?" When children arrive on the marriage scene, nothing is ever the same again—and we wouldn't want it to be.

However, in the new world of parenting, words like *tired*, *exhausted*, and *bummed out* take on new meaning. We hear a lot about the strain parenting places on marriage relationships, but little about how having children can make your marriage better. Yet God in His wisdom placed us in families—a great place to grow a marriage. Check out these family-based marriage enrichers:

- **Children remind us that we're one.** Little ones running around are a continual reminder that in a tangible way, you are *one*. Each time you see your child's toes, you have to admit they are just like Dad's, or that Susie's big smile is a picture of Mom's smile that won you over and still melts your heart.

• **Children foster teamwork.** Parenting definitely calls for a team approach. As young parents, our evenings went better when we helped each other. Claudia tackled the kitchen as Dave bathed and read to our three boys. We both looked for solutions, like when we hired our eleven-year-old neighbor to come over and play with the kids during the "suicide hour"—that hour in the late afternoon when Claudia was on her last legs and trying to get dinner on the table. Just giving your mate a coupon for one hour of "off-duty" solitude can build your marriage team.

• **Children promote appreciation.** Because the responsibilities of parenting leave less free time for two, you'll learn to appreciate each other in a new way. To be alone together is a real treat and one worth working for—which fosters another benefit.

• **Children promote creativity.** You'll think of all kinds of ways to spend time alone, like planning a "Progressive Errand Date." Group your errands together. You can have time alone in the car as you visit the cleaners, post office, drugstore and, on your way home, stop for tea.

• **Children check our communication.** It's amazing what you say or don't say when you remember that little ears are listening. You're the model. It's enough to make us all stop and think before we speak. Just doing that would benefit any marriage. We quickly learned that we needed to be on the same track and say the same thing. Our boys made mincemeat out of us if we were divided.

• **Children keep us honest.** Does our talk match our walk? If not, little eyes will see and report it. You may tell your children it's wrong to lie, but what happens when they hear you say, "Tell him I'm not home" when the phone rings, or when you look the other way when your twelve year old wants to go to a PG-13 movie?

Children need parents who are honest, real, and who admit it when they blow it. We believe our children learned how to ask for forgiveness by observing us. Forgiving and asking for forgiveness are important ingredients in healthy families and healthy marriages.

- **Children prevent boredom**. With children around, something is always going on. You don't have to worry about sitting around in the evening and lamenting, "What should we do tonight?" If you don't have plans, your kids will! Children can also help you relax and loosen up. Every family seems to have one clown who helps to keep things light and unpredictable. Your marriage will be more fun if you learn to laugh with your kids and at yourself.

- **Children give great rewards**. We remember the year we witnessed our youngest son's college graduation. As he and his classmates walked across the stage, a great sigh of relief went up from six hundred sets of college parents.

    It's rewarding to see our children launched into life. And part of that reward is all the memories of how your children enriched your life and marriage. You'll never run out of things to reminisce about.

Chapter II

For Their Own Good!

We'll never forget our first winter getaway at Hilton Head Island in South Carolina. Why would we go to the beach in the winter? With three active kids, it was an accomplishment to pull off a getaway any time of the year. And besides, we like deserted beaches!

We could already envision long walks and talks. Friends were loaning us their condo. The car was packed with our clothes, tennis rackets, books, and groceries.

Just as we were leaving, our son Jonathan complained, "It's not fair! I want to go to Hilton Head, too! You just don't care about me or you would take me with you."

"Jonathan," we responded, "you may not believe this, but we are doing this for your own good." The look on his face confirmed that he didn't believe us.

"One day when you are grown and married and have kids of your own," we continued, "you'll remember that your parents on occasion would take time to be alone together. You'll remember how pleasant and relaxed they were after their little getaways. It'll help you take the initiative to spend time alone with your wife, building your own marriage—even if your kids threaten to never speak to you again and tell you it's just not fair. You can tell them you're doing it for their own good!"

Our friend, Dr. Howard Hendricks, says that one of the

greatest things you can do for your child is to love your child's mother or father. Mom can love the child and Dad can love the child, but if Mom and Dad don't love each other, the child will feel insecure. Our children need to be reassured of our love for each other. It's one priceless gift we can give them.

Over the years, one way we have been able to build our relationship with each other is by taking time out together. A week at Hilton Head Island or in the Colorado Rockies may not be a possibility for you right now. Major vacations require major time and resources. Twenty-four-hour or weekend mini-vacations are easier to pull off. We'll even tell you how.

If you're on a limited budget, consider trading babysitting with another family. Our friend Betty told us how she and Jeff work it out. "We regularly get away one weekend every other month. We swap kids with another family, so every other month we have their children for a weekend. For us, it's really worth it."

If dollars are really tight, you might even trade houses. You spend the weekend alone in another couple's home while they take their kids to your house. This works better if the children in both families are already friends. Let us encourage you to get away from your own home. Otherwise you may spend your time alone doing all those things that need to be done and are easier to do without the children underfoot. You may get much accomplished, but completely miss the purpose of your private time— to deepen your own marital bonds.

Have we inspired you? Put some feet on your inspiration. Set a time when you and your mate can have just a few uninterrupted minutes for planning. Once you're alone, talk about these questions:

1. If money and time were unlimited, where would we like to

go for a just-for-two vacation? (It never
hurts to dream—dreams can brighten any evening!)

2. At this stage of life, what can we pull off realistically?

3. What steps do we need to take to make it happen?

Believe us, your children's future spouses will thank you.
Just recently one of our sons called to tell us about the wonderful weekend he and his wife had at a country bed-and-breakfast.
The Arp tradition continues to the next generation! After all,
isn't that what it's all about?

Chapter 12

Desperately Seeking Soothers

We remember when a good night's sleep was as simple as giving our baby a little rubber device known as a pacifier. All three of our babies were suckers (and their parents were suckers for what worked). Pacifiers even added to our marital bliss, as we were both more pleasant to each other when we got our beauty rest.

We hadn't thought about those "pacifying times" for a few years—until some ducks reminded us. Recently, we slipped away for a cup of cappuccino at a little sidewalk cafe on the edge of a lake. Nearby, watching the ducks with us was a young family, complete with a baby in a stroller, pacifier in mouth.

All was quiet and peaceful—until the baby suddenly decided to feed her pacifier to the ducks. Have you ever seen a duck with a pacifier in its mouth? It's quite a sight! First, mama and papa duck fought over it. Then, the little ducklings got into the act. Each was determined to win the pacifier, which of course was useless to them.

As we laughed, we began to talk about how this picture wasn't really so funny. Don't we often struggle to grasp things just as silly? How much time and energy do we waste chasing useless things that we think will pacify us? It's a fallacy to believe that "the one with the most toys wins." Things never have and never will pacify us. Without realizing it, sometimes we are as silly as those ducks.

The ducks snagged our curiosity, so we decided to look up the definition of *pacifier*. A pacifier is anything that appeases, calms, soothes, tranquilizes, and placates.

What are some of the pacifiers of the nineties? Do you find that your profession or work appeases you? What about the tranquilizing effect of television or sports (or sports on television)? It's common to see young families at the video stores on Friday afternoon checking out an armload of videos for the weekend.

We might also look to other people to sweeten our lives. As important as our children are, they have the potential to become our sole source of significance; before we know it, we find ourselves looking to them to meet our needs.

How many parents live life vicariously through their kids? Are you a dad who wants his son to be the football star, or a mom who hopes her child will get the lead role in the school play? Even in our marriage, we can demand more from our mate than he or she can give.

How can we find balance?

Pascal, the great French scientist, gave us the solution. He wrote that there is a God-shaped vacuum in the heart of every man that can be satisfied by no living thing but only by God, the Creator, made known to us through His son, Jesus Christ. Only in our relationship with Christ can we find true significance, peace, calmness, and the sweet stillness that pacifies our hearts.

Proverbs 4:23 says, "Above all else, guard your heart, for it is the wellspring of life." If we allow God to fill our hearts with His love and peace, we're truly able to enjoy other relationships.

The problem is that our priorities easily get out of whack. While our desire is to put God above all else, we first need to ask: What are our pacifiers? Are they positive or negative? Are they useful? Are they biblical? Are they hindering or helping to build our marriage relationship? Are they good in themselves, but keeping us from investing quality time in our marriage? After you consider these questions thoughtfully, you can make your own plan of action to cut back and simplify your lives.

Do you identify with the ducks? What fruitless goals are you chasing? Find your own quaint sidewalk cafe and, over a couple of cups of cappuccino, talk about the pacifiers in your life.

Chapter 13

Vive la Difference

"Opposites attract," goes the old adage. Is this true in your marriage? What differences still amaze you?

We are very different from each other. Sometimes those differences not only attract us to each other, but they can also create tension in our relationship. For the first few years of our marriage, we each tried changing the other; it just didn't work.

Think back to your pre-marriage days. Remember the first time you ever saw your mate? What attracted you to each other? Claudia still remembers being attracted to this laid-back, easy-going guy who had all the time in the world to listen to her. Dave liked Claudia's high energy level, endless ideas, and constant chatter. It was a great match. Right? Well, yes and no. Yes, before marriage, when romance and hormones abounded! Every day was exciting. Dave's calmness and attentiveness complemented Claudia's three-ring circus of activity. Our rose-tinted glasses helped us appreciate our differences and we naturally seemed to concentrate on the positive.

Then came the wedding and the honeymoon, closely followed by the real-life struggles of a young couple on a limited budget trying to balance work and complete college at the same time. Romance was still present, but reality was its roommate. Claudia redefined Dave's laid-back quality as lack of motivation. No matter how many firecrackers she set under Dave, he was still slow and steady.

Dave couldn't understand why Claudia was so introspective and analytical, and soon tired of this bundle of activity he had married. Oh, for one quiet evening!

Fast-forward eight years. Add a trio of little boys and all the responsibilities of parenting. Life just got more complicated—and our differences more pronounced. About this time we made a job change that required us to take a battery of psychological tests. We still remember the day we filled out those tests. Dave nonchalantly checked off his answers while watching a football game on television. Claudia was intense, cross-checking her answers for "consistency."

The next week we were interviewed by a psychologist, Dr. Blandau. He sat at his desk, looking at our test results. "Dave, here are your strong points." As he listed them, Dave began to feel better and better. He went on, "Here are the areas where you are weak." That wasn't nearly as enjoyable for Dave to hear, but the psychologist was right on target!

Then he went through the same procedure with Claudia, listing her strengths and weaknesses. Looking at both of us he said, "Dave and Claudia, here are the areas you agree on, and here are the areas where you tend to have problems." He could have been a fly on the walls of our home—he didn't miss anything. Then he gave us one of the most beneficial challenges of our lives:

"You've probably noticed, Dave, that your weak areas are Claudia's strengths, and Claudia, your weak areas are Dave's strengths. If you will allow each other to operate in your areas of strength and not be threatened by the other, you have the potential for being a terrific team."

We would like to tell you that we applied his advice instantly.

But we didn't! It's hard to admit openly that your weakness is your mate's strength. It took time and practice—and at times we still struggle—but we continue to take Dr. Blandau's challenge seriously. It's helped us to be a stronger team and it can help you, too!

Take a few minutes to assess your strengths and weaknesses. Batteries of psychological tests aren't necessary. Instead, simply start by talking about the ways you are different from each other. For example, you may be spontaneous and like to let family life just happen, while your mate is a detailed planner and likes a lot of structure in each day.

Next talk about the ways you are alike. Maybe you have similar values and a common faith in God. Perhaps you are both private people and would rather talk facts than feelings.

Do you already see areas where your differences give balance to your marriage team? Is there an area where you are so similar that you need to compensate? For instance, if you're both the serious type, how can you add a little humor and fun?

Our goal is to benefit from each other's strengths and appreciate each other's differences. Take it from us, this is one goal worth working toward.

Years later we took the same tests again and sat down with the same psychologist. The results? We had actually learned from each other. Our weak areas weren't as weak. We had learned to work together as a team, plus we definitely were having more fun.

Now, we challenge you to prove it for yourself. Work for unity in your diversity, and you too can say, *"Vive la différence!"*

Chapter 14

What the Paper Place Mat Said

Is it time for your marriage checkup? If you're thinking "What's that?" then it's time for sure! In fact, we suggest that every couple, no matter how long you've been married, take an annual marriage checkup. What better time than now to make sure you're on track in your marriage!

A marriage checkup isn't expensive or complicated. You don't have to make an appointment months in advance, spend hours in a waiting room, or have your weight recorded. It's simply looking at your marriage as it is today and making minor adjustments for the future. Adjustments you make in the hectic parenting years can make a significant difference in your marriage relationship when you have an empty nest.

We had one such checkup on the way home from an evening church service. Our pastor had challenged us with II Timothy 4:7, where Paul writes that he had fought the good fight and finished the race. Over two glasses of iced tea and one shared order of potato skins, we talked about what we wanted our marriage to look like at the "end of our race."

On the back of our paper place mat we jotted down the positive things about our marriage team. Our list included good communication, the ability to laugh, and mutual commitment to our three sons. (We remember because we saved that place mat!) Then we agreed on two action points: to work more diligently at sharing our parenting responsibilities, and to schedule more fun times together. We chose a time that next week to play tennis.

First, Get Serious

All you need for your checkup are two pens, some paper, and an hour or so of peace and quiet. Start by answering the following questions. You may want to write out your answers separately, and then discuss them together.

1. What do I like most about my mate? (For instance, Claudia would answer that she likes Dave's easygoing personality and listening ear.)

2. What was the best thing that happened to us as a couple in the last twelve months?

3. If my mate had the power to change one thing about me, what do I think he or she would change? (Claudia is sure Dave would answer that she could be neater—especially with the horizontal files on her desk.)

4. Now write down five things you'd like to do together with your mate in the next year. (Dave's list would include getting our home office organized or escaping for a week alone in the mountains or at the beach, while Claudia would include writing a new book and continuing our daily walks together.)

As you enjoy reflecting on the past twelve months of your marriage, set goals for the next year. Combine your lists of things you would like to do together and set priorities. Choose a time and place to accomplish your top priority. During the next year, work your way through as much of your combined list as possible.

Then, Plan for Fun

We sometimes feel guilty if we aren't doing two things at once—and super guilty when we are having fun together and haven't included our children. But remember, relationships are built in twos. Children need well-balanced, happy parents who enjoy being together. We don't know one couple who at the time of their divorce were having fun together. Fun times together aren't optional—they're critical to your marital health!

So take our prescription. Set aside time for your marriage checkup. This may be just the first of many annual checkups you actually look forward to.

Chapter 15

Gas Wars

Our all-time favorite car, a '92 Oldsmobile, dubbed "Lumbar" for her orthopedic, adjustable seats, has an interesting gas gauge. We can drive for miles on the first half tank—but then go from half-full to empty in record time.

On a recent trip when Lumbar reached the half-full, half-empty mark, Claudia asked, "Dave, do we need to get gas?"

Dave didn't perceive her question as nagging until she had repeated it three times. You see, there was a gas war going on, and gas was one or two cents per gallon cheaper at each station we passed. Dave just continued driving, looking for a better deal.

"You'd better stop," Claudia finally insisted. "The price is starting to go back up."

Still the stubborn driver kept driving, and the persistent co-pilot kept insisting. Our moods turned grim. Then it happened. Prices were five cents, then ten cents more per gallon.

Unfortunately, we paid a much higher price that day than just the extra two dollars for a tank of gas. Because we each wanted our own way, it also cost us our team spirit.

Pushing for our own way is not the way to build a Christian marriage. A strong marriage is built on the biblical principles Jesus demonstrated:

- Jesus modeled servanthood. He said, "The first shall be last and the last shall be first," and that it is "more blessed to give than receive." He washed His disciples' feet. But do we model servanthood in marriage? Or do we want the other to wash the dishes, fill up the car with gas, answer the phone, or bathe the kids and read the night-night story?

- Jesus modeled acceptance. He initiated the conversation with the Samaritan woman at the well. He didn't criticize the weird way John the Baptist dressed. How are we at accepting our mates? How do you respond if your mate's hair is a bit too short or too long? Or what if your mate has a few extra pounds for you to love? Should little irritations be that irritating?

- Jesus modeled unconditional love. That's I Corinthians 13 love, which is patient and kind and hardly notices when the other does wrong. In twentieth-century jargon, that means you hardly notice the topless tube of toothpaste, or the grass that needs mowing when it's not your turn, or the family van that resembles your baby's playpen. Love means being patient with each other when the bank balance is uncomfortably low. It means finding ways to love each other on less instead of complaining.

When we think back on our gas-gauge experience, we realize we weren't following Christ's example. We were missing God's best deal—which has absolutely nothing to do with the price of gas. We were prime examples of how not to have marital harmony. And we were missing the fun of the trip.

What did we learn from our experience? One is to keep a full tank of gas. Our "spiritual gas" is the Word of God and time spent in prayer and meditation with the Lord. We can't go through our hectic day as parents and partners without filling our tank. Perhaps it's time to stop, refocus, and ask the Lord to give us a full tank of love and grace. Ask Him to fill your partner's tank, too.

Now, when Lumbar's gas gauge hits the halfway mark, we look for the nearest station. Well, maybe the second-nearest—you never know if gas might be two cents cheaper over the hill or around the bend!

Chapter 16

The Rumor Is Humor

If a man insisted always on being serious, and never allowed himself a bit of fun and relaxation, he would go mad or become unstable without knowing it.

—Herodotus, The History of Herodotus, Book II

When thinking about adding fun to our marriage, we added a new mentor couple, Dave and Jeanie Stanley. They believe every couple can add more laughter and joy to their marriage relationship. We had the delightful experience of meeting Dave and Jeanie when we were keynote speakers at the United Marriage Encounter International Celebration. The Stanleys were our hosts, and from the time they picked us up at the airport, we could see that this couple—married for more than forty-five years with four children and two grandchildren—had a special spark of love for each other. What was their secret?

Our curiosity got the best of us, so one afternoon when we weren't giving a presentation, we attended their workshop "What Now, My Love?" where they shared how they keep playfulness and fun in their marriage.

Foundation for Fun

The Stanleys said that the basis of the joy in their marriage is their relationship with God. They start each day with wake-up prayer as they snuggle in bed. They like to pray when they are walking and often kneel in prayer together. They also read Scripture together and share their feelings with each other. This practice provides the foundation for their fun and fascinating ideas. You're going to love these jewels! Here are our favorites.

1. They have pet names for each other, and not just two or three. They have hundreds and seem to add more daily. One of their pet names is "Lover Bunnies." There's a reason; they love rabbits and have four (the stuffed variety) that always travel with them.

2. They look for ways to give each other compliments. "As plants need water," they shared, "we need affirmation from each other."

3. They write each other love letters.

4. They have their own special kisses. "Romance depends on your attitude and perspective," they say.

5. They plan regular dates (a couple after our own hearts).

6. They handle conflict with a light touch. They have a ten-minute silence rule. At any time, either can call for ten minutes of silence. If nonverbal communication is a problem, they also have an out of sight for ten minutes rule. This helps them to calm down and get things back in perspective.

7. At airports, they fake good-bye kisses and then get on the plane together.

8. At grocery store checkout counters, Dave asks Jeanie to marry him all over again! Jeanie enthusiastically says, "Yes!"

9. They affectionately tease each other, but they are never unkind. Also, they are careful to avoid vulnerable spots.

They look for things to laugh about and don't take themselves too seriously.

10. They have shared goals that are bigger than they are. Together they have committed themselves to specific goals; one is to strengthen marriages.

The Way It Used to Be

We asked Jeanie and Dave how they kept their love alive back in the early parenting years. Here's what they told us:

"From the very beginning of our marriage, we had fun together, and though parenting brought many adjustments—for instance, with two toddlers eighteen months apart, we didn't camp out in pup tents anymore—we did look for ways to find our fun moments."

"Sometimes we would put our children to bed early and grab time just for us for a late dinner or a game of double solitaire. We've always walked together and have bypassed television. The latter definitely benefited our children. We logged many family evenings reading together and playing games. One way we kept our own sense of fun and sanity was having fun together with our children."

Dave and Jeanie, we salute you and thank you for being such fun role models for us and many other couples.

Chapter 17

Grow the Distance

Grow old along with me!
The best is yet to be.
—Robert Browning

Do these words ring true for you? Parenting can certainly age us, but is life getting better? Perhaps you can't see past potty training, reading books about Madeline, and picking up Duplo® blocks.

Or maybe the preschool years are history. Your elementary-aged children actually talk to you and like to have you at their soccer games and piano recitals. Things are improving, but just as you think you see light at the end of the tunnel, you discover it's that fast-approaching train called adolescence! Each stage of parenting puts stress on a marriage. Sleepless nights with babies (and teens), bickering among siblings, and the everyday hassles of family life tested our patience with our sons and with each other. But with God's help, we hung in there. You can too.

Our Marriage Secret

What keeps love growing over the years? One secret is building the right foundation. Genesis 2:24 tells us, "For this cause a man shall leave his father and mother, and shall cleave to his wife, and they shall become one flesh" (NASB). Consider these three principles:

Leaving: The first step in having a Bible-based marriage is leaving our parents and focusing on our mate. Then, daily, we make choices to leave other things that grab our attention. It may be as simple as turning off the TV, or as complicated as planning a weekend getaway for two without the kids. What do you need to leave so that you can refocus on your mate?

Cleaving: This means sticking together during the hard times as well as the good. Our boys were masters at the "divide and conquer" game. They knew who to ask for what. Generally, as parents, we stuck together, but at times our kids were too clever. They knew Dad was the risk-taker and would probably say yes to questions like, "Can we go rock climbing? It's only raining a little bit." Mom, on the other hand, would shriek, "You want to do what?"

Do you present a united front? Do you stick up for one another—even when you'd rather not? Do your kids know if Mom says no, Dad won't say yes?

Becoming One: God created us male and female and put the potential for passion within us. He designed us to experience a unique oneness with our spouse. It is with God's blessing that we pursue loving our mate. Remember, that's how we became parents in the first place!

How are you living out Genesis 2:24? How does your role as parent affect your role as partner? Is there something you need to leave? Do you stick together when life's hard? What can you do this week to "romance your mate"?

Finish the Race

Paul writes, "I have fought the good fight, I have finished the race, I have kept the faith" (II Tim. 4:7).

To go the distance in marriage, we need to follow Paul's example. We need to live out our faith. We need to pace ourselves and persevere to the end of life's race. What do you want your marriage to look like at the finish line?

Find a Mentor

For years, David and Vera Mace have been our friends and models. On their fortieth anniversary they founded the Association for Couples in Marriage Enrichment. They worked together tirelessly over the fifty-seven years of their marriage to help couples strengthen their marriages.

If you build your marriage on God's Word, picture what you want your marriage to be at the finish line, and find a mentor, you'll leave a legacy of love to the next generation. You'll be able to say the words of poet Robert Browning:

Grow old along with me!
The best is yet to be,
The last of life for which the first was made;
Our times are in His hand
Who saith: 'A whole I planned—
Youth shows but half; trust God, see all nor be afraid.'

Chapter 18

Mad About You

Never trust a person who says he doesn't get angry. Anger is common to the human race, and there are no relationships that have as much potential for producing anger as those in a marriage and family!

Think about the last time you were angry. Was it when Jenny made mud pies after she was all dressed for church? When the clothes Kim was supposed to put in the dryer mildewed? When your teenage driver returned your car with the gas gauge on empty? When your mate was late again and didn't call?

A Mountaintop Experience

On a recent trip to Switzerland we had a memorable anger experience. We went to Engelberg, a little village in the Swiss Alps, where we used to go hiking as a family when our boys were young. Memories abounded! Especially the time our family took a cogged railroad to the top of one of the mountains, then walked down a gentle path with an incredible view of the valley—complete with Swiss cows ringing their bells. We were eager to repeat the experience, minus three boys.

The cogged railroad had been replaced by a cable car. No problem—until we tried to figure out where to get off. Claudia thought the first stop was it. Dave insisted it was the second, which we quickly discovered was 1,000 meters above the village.

Oh well, it would just take a little longer to get back down to the village. We happy hikers set off on what we thought was the easy way down.

The first thirty minutes were great. But then the gentle path took a drastic turn—it looked like a rock climber's delight. As we searched for our easy path, we got off the trail and came to a sheer drop-off. We started to get angry.

Our dilemma: How could we turn our anger into creative energy to find a solution? Fortunately, on that day we remembered to make anger our friend. Marriage specialists David and Vera Mace say that the biggest problem in marriage is not lack of communication, but the inability to handle and process anger. They remind us that anger is a normal, healthy emotion. However, once angry, we are responsible for what we do about it. Venting or suppressing anger only makes matters worse. The Bible tells us not to let the sun go down on our anger, but to acknowledge that we do need to do something about it!

Make Anger Work for You

The Maces suggest that a better way to handle anger is to process it. They developed a three-step system for doing just that. We've used it over the years, and you can, too. Choose to use anger creatively for growth in your marriage by agreeing to take these action steps:

1. Acknowledge your anger to each other as soon as you become aware of it.
2. Renounce the "right" to vent anger at each other. It's okay to say something like, "I'm getting angry with you, but you know I'm not going to attack you." This way, the other person doesn't have to be defensive.
3. Ask for the other's help in dealing with the anger. If your

partner is angry with you and appeals
to you to help clear it up, it is definitely in your
interest to cooperate.

We find that our anger agreement commits us to work on each angry situation that develops between us until we clear it up.

Back to Our Cliff-hanger

There on the cliff edge, Claudia said, "Dave, I need to tell you I'm getting angry with you. We should have gotten off at the first stop. How are we going to get down off this mountain? Where is the trail?"

By not attacking each other, we could work together to find the trail (which, by the way, did include steep, rocky inclines). Three hours later, when we finally came to the trail we'd taken years ago with our sons, we were still friends and could enjoy it!

Our Challenge to You

Discuss the following with your mate and sign the agreement:
Whenever one of us becomes angry:

1. We will acknowledge our anger to each other as soon as we become aware of it.
2. We will not vent anger at each other.
3. We will ask for each other's help in dealing with the anger that has developed.

Signed _____

Signed _____

Take it from us—you can make anger a friend at your house. It may work so well, you'll want to introduce this concept to your kids! We wouldn't leave home—or climb down a mountain—without it.

Chapter 19

A Season to Invest

There is a time for everything, and a season
for every activity under heaven.
—Ecclesiastes 3:1

Time—what is it? Sixty seconds make a minute, minutes turn into hours, and hours into days. Time zips by almost unnoticed. Then something happens and time seems to stand still. You see time in a new perspective and life is never the same again.

It was one of those phone calls you dread. Lillian, Dave's mom, had suffered a stroke. In the next few weeks as Lillian lingered between life and death, time stopped long enough for us to reflect on this wonderful lady and the seasons of her life and marriage.

Dave's parents were married for fifty-five wonderful years. That's long in today's world, but even lifelong marriages at some point come to an end. As Dave's parents' marriage came to an end, we had to pause and ask ourselves, "Are we being good stewards of the time we still have together?" Perhaps you'll want to reflect on the same question.

How are you investing your marriage moments? Each season of marriage comes with different stress points and challenges. What season are you in? Have the casual discovery days of the first months and years of your marriage accelerated into the hectic and hassling years of toddlers and preschoolers? Cheerios® wars, peanut butter on doorknobs, and wall-to-wall Legos® don't especially promote marital togetherness. Time out together is more likely spent at T-ball, soccer practice, or swim meets. You may even close your telephone conversations with "Bye-bye." (A habit we've never been able to break!)

Perhaps it's time to take some "time out" for your marriage. Dave's parents did. He remembers that when he was a young boy, his parents went off alone together from time to time. As a teenager, he loved catching his mom and dad hugging and kissing on the balcony. As empty nesters, his parents were each other's best friend. Throughout the seasons of their marriage, they modeled to us what an enriched marriage looks like. And through Lillian's death, we are reminded that our time here is limited. How are we investing the time we do have? What are we modeling to our own children?

Here's our challenge to you. Take time today to talk about the seasons of your marriage. Ask yourself, "Are we investing the moments we do have in growing together and loving each other?" If your marriage time-account is low, plan one thing you can do together. Try one of these ideas, or invent your own. Be creative.

- If you have a new baby, enjoy snacks by candlelight after the late-night feeding when all—okay, almost all—is calm.
- Take that hour when the kids are at soccer or T-ball practice to walk around the field or track. It's a great time to talk.
- During the teen years, go out for an early-morning breakfast date.
- Take the weekly trip to the grocery store together. Sipping

a free sample of gourmet coffee while
you cross items off your list is also another great opportunity to talk.

- Take ten minutes before bed each night to pray together.
  Keep a prayer log of the seasons of your marriage.

Invest in your marriage each season, and you'll pass on a
legacy of love.

The sadness of Lillian's passing was softened by another
phone call: our son's voice saying, "Hi Grandma! Hi Grandpa!"
ushered in a new season in our marriage. Our first grandchild,
Sophia Marie Arp, entered this world and has enriched ours!
Grandchildren bring a new motivation to be a positive model
both in our marriage and in our personal lives. What will we
pass on to Sophie? What are you passing on to your children
and future grandchildren? The legacy of a healthy, loving, growing Christian marriage is ours to give to the next generation.
Take time to think about that!

Chapter 20

Quiet, Please!

"Our kids were never that loud!" Claudia commented as the noise level on our jam-packed flight went up a couple of decibels.

Dave responded, "You just don't remember." It's true. Over time, memory fades. But there was something distinctly familiar in the roar of little voices being used to capacity.

Have you noticed the unspoken bond among parents who have ever traveled with their children—especially on airplanes? "Noise on planes doesn't bother me," one dad commented. "I have three kids at home and I can't concentrate unless there's a roar in the background!"

Whether traveling or at home, if you have children, you have a noise factor to deal with. Add the excitement of holidays or a special event, and your family noise level (or roar) may rise to an even higher pitch. How can you and your spouse tune out the noise and tune into each other? How can you find quiet times together in the whirlwind of holiday activities? These proactive steps work for us.

We make lists—lots of lists. Our lists help us focus, simplify our lives, and find quiet times for two. For instance:

- We make a list of what we are not going to do. We will not fill our family calendar to the brim!
- We list our blessings. In the quietness of our hearts we want to acknowledge and give thanks to our loving heavenly Father who has guided, directed, and protected us individually, as a couple, and as a family. You might try one

of our traditions, the "Thankful Box." Place a box or bowl on your dining-room table, complete with pen and notepaper. Whenever you think of a blessing, write it down, fold it, and place it in your Thankful Box. Then at family mealtimes once a week, read to each other from your box of blessings. Or, if you don't think you can maintain the tradition the whole year, you might start a "Thankful Box" on Thanksgiving Day and read your blessings on Christmas Eve, Christmas Day, or New Year's Eve.

- We make a "quiet times for two" list. We've done this at Christmastime as well, remembering Mary and how she took time to "ponder in her heart" all that was happening that first Christmas. In the same way, we want to ponder together the true significance of that historic event. Reading through the Gospel of Luke helps us do that. While a daily quiet time for two is a noble goal, it may not be realistic. We suggest choosing maybe one or two times each week that will be your quiet time for two. Perhaps this is the year to memorize the Christmas story.

- One of our most important lists is our simplicity list. It includes quiet activities we can do together. It might include a nighttime walk to look at the stars or a weekly lunch date.

A simple way we add a little quietness is each evening we turn down the lights, light candles, and play a praise tape or CD. For ten minutes we are silent. It's a great way to calm overstimulated, lively little ones.

Now it's your turn! We challenge you to grab a few quiet minutes and make your own lists. When you simplify and focus, you may find the roar of family life is a happy noise that someday will be a great memory.

Chapter 21

Date
Your Mate

"What's your most fun date?" we asked Phil and Cindy, parents of two young boys.

Now Phil and Cindy are a fun couple, so our pen was poised to record their answer when Cindy responded, "You mean before we got married?" Not exactly what we had in mind!

We asked another fun couple for their dating experiences and they told us about their attempted big date. They went to a nice local hotel for an extravagant getaway and ended up in a room by the ice machine where a college fraternity party was setting a record for noise production. It was so loud that in the middle of the night they packed up, checked out, and went back to their relatively quiet home.

It wasn't that our friends hadn't tried dating, but both couples confessed that outside of dates to soccer practices, baseball games, and swim meets, they had actually done little dating in the past few years.

Why is it so hard to date your mate? And with all the hassles, why even try? We believe dating helps keep the life and fun in a marriage.

On a recent television talk show, a marriage specialist said that many view marriage as death, boredom, or the end of the line. God forbid! He created marriage to be a permanent bond of love and commitment between husband and wife—to be both lovers and friends through the days of our lives. He didn't create marriage to be the end of the line. Still, some people view it in such negative terms. But why?

Having worked with married couples for many years, we have our own opinion. We believe life goes out of a marriage when the couple stops working on it. And when a couple stops working on their marriage, it means they've stopped having fun together. Show us a marriage that is faltering and we'll show you a marriage where the fun is gone.

So how can you put some fun back into your marriage? You can start by dating your mate. Dating may be something you did before you got married or before you had children, but isn't in your marriage vocabulary today.

The good news is it's easy to do something about it. Start by carving out some "just-me-and-my-mate" time to explore the possibilities. Together, make a list of fun things you would like to do together—anything from an overnight getaway to learning to wallpaper to a walking-and-talking date. Some other fun dates you might want to consider:*

- **Formal-Dinner-in-the-Park Date**. Put on your black tie or evening gown and grab the picnic basket for an evening under the stars!
- **I'm-Just-Too-Tired Date**. Put the kids to bed early, order take out, turn on the answering machine, and then just relax and enjoy each other.
- **Photo Date**. Go to your favorite haunt and snap away. Borrow a camera with a timer so you can be in the photos together. Then simply set the timer and run back and smile!
- **Gourmet-Cooking Date**. Have you ever wanted to take up gourmet cooking? Think about learning it together and

call it a date! Plan the menu, grocery shop together at an upscale market, and cook your dinner together!

- **Yellow-Road, Blue-Highway Date**. Choose a fifty-mile radius around your home and see what you can discover. No fast food or four-lane roads allowed.
- **Workout Date**. Get in shape together at a health club. Or, if the budget is tight, walk or jog together.
- **Home-Depot Date**. Go to a local home-improvement store and dream about remodeling projects you'd like to tackle or have done someday.
- **Window-Shopping Date**. Go when the stores are closed and it will be a guaranteed cheap date. Instead of dreaming about what you would like to have, pick out all the things in the window you already have.
- **Airport Date**. Go to the airport and watch people come and go. Pretend you are saying good-bye to each other and hug and kiss passionately! Then move to another part of the airport and pretend you are meeting each other after a long absence. Run into each other's arms!
- **Proposal Date**. Go to a public place and ask your mate to marry you all over again!

Now choose one, pick a time, and write down what you must do to make it happen—like find a sitter, save the money, or clear your overcommitted schedule. Start with a date that will be easy to pull off.

Will dating make a difference in your marriage? Our answer is an emphatic "Yes!" If you don't believe us, ask Fred and Nancy. Here's what they wrote us:

"Thank you for sharing your dating ideas. My husband and I have a lot of fun in our marriage and it is legal, moral, inexpensive, and biblical. We know we can't take our marriage for granted, so we continue to search for reinforcements such as your books and articles."

Fred and Nancy have taken the initiative to make their marriage come alive with fun, laughter, and good times together. Now the ball is in your court. Go on and have a great time. Have a date with your mate.

*Adapted from: David and Claudia Arp, *52 Dates for You and Your Mate* (Nashville: Thomas Nelson, 1993).

Chapter 22

Bless This House

Knee-deep in doorknobs, paint chips, and carpet samples, we looked at each other and asked, "Are we having fun yet?" It all started with an innocent Sunday afternoon drive. But before we could say "low interest rates" three times fast, we were on the move.

Moving isn't new for us—we've made thirteen major moves. With each came opportunities to forbear with each other and to trust God with change. While our most traumatic move was to Europe with only six-weeks' notice and three kids ages six, four, and fifteen months—need we say more—our recent move across town was not without stress! Moving, for a parent, is what giving up a security blanket is for a toddler. It's not easy to let go of the familiar. But moving can also be a great time to reaffirm your commitment to your marriage, your family, and to God.

If you've ever moved, you can appreciate the unsettling process of getting settled into a new home. But what makes a house a home is not the furniture or the floor plan—what defines *home* is the living and loving that take place inside. Solomon gives sage advice in Proverbs 24:3,4 for doing just that: "By wisdom a house is built, and through understanding it is established; through knowledge its rooms are filled with rare and beautiful treasures."

We don't think Solomon was talking about filling our houses

with the latest trends in furniture, knick-knacks, or stuff; so as we considered our move, we wanted our new home to be filled with God's love.

When the movers and packing boxes were history and we were reasonably settled, we asked God's special blessing on our home and those who would live and visit within these walls. With our family and close friends and led by our pastor, we dedicated our new home. You can to do the same—whether you have lived in your home for ten days or ten years. It makes no difference if you live in a one-room apartment, a condo, or a three-story house. (We've found that you can get clean in all sizes of bathrooms and that dustballs are no respecters of square footage!)

You may want to plan a formal occasion like we did, and include loved ones and your pastor—or you could choose a family night and bless your house together with your children. This can be a time of recommitment both to your marriage and to your children. What a great way to pass on a godly heritage! As you pray, consider including things such as:

Welcome-Mat Wishes

Begin outside your front door, and thank God for your marriage, family, and home. Pray that your home will reflect your love for Him, for one another, for family and neighbors, and that this place will be an outpost of God's kingdom. Affirm verses like "Unless the Lord builds the house, its builders labor in vain" (Ps. 127:1), and "May the Lord bless you from Zion all the days of your life . . . may you live to see your children's children" (Ps. 128:5,6). Together ask for God's peace to be granted to all who enter. Then open the door and enter.

In the Living Room

Pray that in this room your family will have eyes and ears open to God, to one another, and to those who will come to share your lives, enjoy your company, and seek your wisdom; that you can rejoice with those who rejoice and weep with those who weep. And in the quiet hours, that you may know the pleasure of His presence. Then ask God to fill this room with His presence.

In the Kitchen

Thank God for giving you good things to eat and for blessing your fellowship around the table. Pray that the meals prepared and eaten in this place will remind you of His bountiful mercy, love, and grace. Then ask Him to fill this room with His presence.

In the Master Bedroom

Acknowledge how Christ has pursued us with His love. Pray that in this room you will celebrate your love as a married couple, and that you will also find rest and renewal in sleep. Now ask God to fill this room with His loving presence.

As you continue through the other rooms in your house, ask God to bless and fill every nook and cranny with His love and peace. You may want to write specific prayers for your children's bedrooms. After you have blessed each room, gather again in the living room for a closing prayer. You may want to use our closing liturgy:

Leader: Now Father, Son, and Holy Spirit, sanctify this house;

People: For everything in heaven and on earth is yours.

Leader: Yours, Lord, is the kingdom;

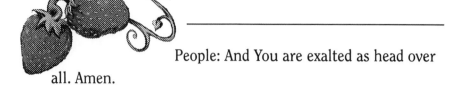

People: And You are exalted as head over all. Amen.

Note: For the complete house blessing we used, refer to Appendix II. You are welcome to adapt it to bless your own home.

Chapter 23

Back-Road Treks

We both like shortcuts, but we've discovered that sometimes they're not marriage builders. One evening, a shortcut in the East Tennessee mountains tested our patience. We are usually travel smart and know our respective jobs. Dave drives. Claudia navigates. We typically like to explore those little-used blue roads on the map, but on this foggy, stormy evening we were tired and simply wanted a shortcut home.

When we came to a fork in the road, we were stumped. Both of our options were dirt roads. Of course, there were no road signs. Our outdated map didn't help. Glaring at each other in total frustration, we realized we had two choices. We could continue to blame each other. "Why can't you find us on that map? Are you reading it upside down?" "You're the one who wanted to take this shortcut. Why didn't you listen to me?"

Or we could turn our *why* and *you* statements into *I* statements. "I'm sorry I attacked you." "I don't like being lost and I'm a little scared."

Have you ever noticed that *why* questions and *you* statements don't build marriages? They both tend to attack, so we try to avoid them.

Since the road we were on was more like a cow path with no future, we turned around and tried to retrace our tracks. After several tries, we found a landmark we recognized and eventually arrived home. Fortunately, we were still friends; we stopped blaming each other and acknowledged that life involves getting lost once in a while.

Building a marriage while parenting our children reminds us of our late-night mountain adventure. At times you feel lost and out-of-control. Every family experiences those detours and interruptions—like when your child says, "You just don't love me, I'm going to run away from home!" or "It all started when Sally hit me back!" or "I hate going to Sunday school!" or "I'm not eating this yucky food!"

If you and your spouse ever feel disoriented, it may mean you are growing together in your marriage. First, it means you're taking risks. We could have stayed on the interstate that night and had an uneventful, dull trip home. If we don't venture out from time to time, life can become quite boring! What have you done recently that was out of character or adventuresome? Maybe it's time to break out of your routine.

Second, when we feel out of control, we're encouraged to turn to God and ask for help. It's an opportunity to demonstrate our faith and trust in a God who never loses us! Sometimes we see evidence of God working in our families. If we're honest, other times we don't see it. Our challenge is to trust Him in the dark and when we're disoriented, as well as when it's all sunshine.

Third, when we admit we aren't perfect and give ourselves permission to be less than perfect, our children see that we are real. Children learn how to deal with unplanned and frustrating situations by watching their parents.

Recently on a clear summer day, we took the same mountain road. On that day we saw the reflection of the mountains on a crystal-clear lake, and the wildflowers seemed to wave to us in the cool summer breeze. There was plenty of "local color" as we rode by the Bobbie Socks Drive-In, not far from Turnip Town Creek. On that day we were glad we gave adventure another chance. Two totally different experiences on the very same road. But isn't that life?

Take the risk. Don't miss the surprises up the road. Enjoy them together!

Chapter 24

A Marriage Prescription

We've been accused of having too much fun in our marriage. We happily plead guilty! But there are some more serious things we do to maintain our marriage health. For example, taking an annual physical examination.

Actually we detest getting physicals, but each year it's one gift we give to each other. When they're over and the doctor pronounces us well for another year, we're overjoyed and leave with a sense of well-being. We're better spouses when we're healthy.

To lessen the pain when the time for our physicals rolls around, we do them together. But we do have ground rules: No peeking when the other is on the scales. No gloating when one's blood work gets done first. Physicals even reveal some of our differences. For instance, Dave goes to sleep during his EKG while Claudia breathes slowly to relax and lower her elevated blood pressure!

Marriages also need regular checkups. Without proper care and attention, marriages can deteriorate. So wise couples invest in marital physicals which pay rich dividends. Just as you are relieved when pronounced healthy for another year, you can have that same confidence that your marriage is growing and will go the distance.

So, though it may not be your most fun adventure, we, "the marriage doctors," prescribe a marriage checkup. And, unlike physical exams, this can be enjoyable. You don't need a doctor, and you can design your own examination. We suggest checking four areas: physical, mental, spiritual, and practical. You can use the following questions to get you started.

Your Physical Relationship

- On a scale of one to ten (ten being "Wow!"), how would you rate your love life?
- Do you need to plan more regular times alone as a couple? (With young kids around, trust us—if you don't plan, it won't happen!)
- What expectations are realistic at this stage of family life?

Your Mental Connection

Which of the following statements describes your intellectual pursuits together?

- In the last twelve months, we have read and discussed several books.
- We occasionally have adult conversations without interruptions (probably feasible only if you get a sitter and leave the house).
- I haven't used baby talk for the last twenty-four hours.

Your Spiritual Oneness

- Are you closer to each other and to God than you were a year ago?
- Has your prayer life together become more meaningful?
- Can you identify some areas to target for spiritual growth (such as prayer, couple and/or family devotions, giving generously to those in need)?

Your Practical Thoughtfulness

- Do you practice little acts of kindness?
- Do you willingly get up in the middle of the night and say, "Honey, go back to sleep, I'll get up with the baby and comfort her. I know her ears hurt."
- Do you encourage your mate when the bank account is low and your mother-in-law is coming to visit?
- Do you volunteer to clean the toilet when Tommy threw up in it? (If so, you get a ten in this area. You are a "Wow!" spouse.)

As you summarize these four areas, talk about what is right with your marriage. What areas need improvement? Choose one area to concentrate on and then follow our prescription.

Prescription for a Healthy Marriage

Take daily vitamins. Compliments and "I love you's" will enrich any marriage.

Exercise your vocal cords. "Communication tennis" is great exercise. Pick a subject and see how long you can keep the conversation going without answering yes or no.

Maintain a healthy diet. Food for thought, food for the spirit, tea-and-conversation-time for two, and praying together will keep your marriage healthy.

Why should you have marital checkups and take our prescription seriously? Because life will be more fun, and you'll provide a good model for your children. And while it's good for your spouse, your friends, and your extended family, most of all, it's good for you!

Chapter 25

A Holidaze Game Plan

It's easy to feel stressed during the "holidaze" season. Remember when Christmas used to occur just in December? Now it gets earlier each year. Christmas lists appear on refrigerator doors before school starts in the fall. Whatever happened to kids who sang, "All I want for Christmas is my two front teeth?" Green and red decorations hit the stores in early October.

It's easy to feel stressed. Instead of peace on earth and good will toward men, you're caught in a frenzied cycle of working, spending, and preparing that accelerates each day. Then comes the letdown as fatigue, unpaid bills and guilt surface.

Maintain your marriage in the midst of such utter chaos? You've got to be kidding!

We admit, this isn't the easiest time of the year to enrich your marriage. But it is a critical one. There's a reason marriage counselors are overloaded in January. But you don't have to be a holidaze casualty. Consider our three-point Christmas game plan:

Pray

A powerful resource in a Christian marriage is prayer. God tells us that if we lack wisdom, we are to ask and He will give it to us—liberally (James 1:5). We began the habit of praying together after becoming parents—having three boys in five years got us on our knees fast! And over the years we've continued to set aside time to pray together.

Do you pray together? Maybe you're hesitant, shy, or reserved. Or maybe you don't know how to get started. Now is a great time to start—during the holidays it's easy to identify prayer concerns. Start by scheduling time to begin. Maybe you can find time after the kids are in bed or early in the morning before the kids get up. You may even hire a baby-sitter and go off alone on a prayer date. You could:

- Read a favorite passage of Scripture together.
- Talk about how God has led you in the past year and how He has answered your prayers.
- Make a holiday prayer list for each other and for your children.
- Most importantly, actually pray together.

So that the more verbal partner will not monopolize the prayer time, take turns praying one sentence at a time.

As Christian families, we should stress the spiritual side of life all twelve months of the year, not only in November and December.

Plan

Here's a radical approach—first, plan what you're not going to do. This alone is a great marriage enricher. For instance, you are not going to give up time alone with your spouse; you're not going to spend money you don't have; you're not going to overextend your schedule.

One couple sent the following "non-party invitations" to their friends. "If we were going to have a Christmas party, we would invite you to our home on Saturday, from 6 to 10 P.M. But since we aren't having a party this year, we will be home enjoying the time with our family and hope you will do the same.

Let's get together in January. Have a wonder-ful Christmas!"

Take a Tradition Inventory as well. List family traditions, and then ask, "Which ones are meaningful?" We used to have creamed celery each Thanksgiving until we realized no one liked it. Which traditions require more than they deliver?

Only keep or add traditions that are meaningful and doable for your family. One tradition to make permanent each year is to plan time alone with your mate. It'll help you persevere when your household feels like a zoo.

Punt

It helps if you're flexible and willing to punt when things don't go as planned. When the unexpected happens, try one of the following "punters":

- Wear a false nose to the dinner table.
- Give each other a back rub with warm oil.
- Build a fire, turn on soft music, and have a cup of eggnog.
- Make angels in the snow.
- Read a fun book to each other. Every Christmas we pull out *Where the Sidewalk Ends* by Shel Silverstein.

Guard your "team time" with your mate. Pray together, plan together—and when necessary, punt together. When the holi-days are over, you'll find you not only survived, you actually scored another win for your marriage team!

Chapter 26

Languages of Love

We continually discover new ways to embarrass ourselves and keep ourselves humble. But one experience tops them all! For a number of years we lived and worked in Germany and Austria. It didn't take long to discover that the whole world does not speak English and if we wanted to be effective in our work, we simply had to learn the language.

If you've ever learned a second language, you know that this is much easier said than done. Learning German turned out to be one of the biggest challenges of our lives, but we were determined. We took advantage of every opportunity to practice our developing language skills.

During our first year in Inzlingen, Germany, we were invited to a formal garden party. Our German ability at that point could be compared to the language pattern of a two-year-old toddler—it wasn't pretty, but we were beginning to communicate. Or so we thought.

We knew we might be in trouble when our hostess sat us at opposite ends of the long banquet table. The other guests encouraged our language development by only speaking German with us, so we were each on our own. It was a cool German evening and Dave, concerned about Claudia getting chilled, asked her in a loud voice, *"Bist du Kalt?"* The literal translation is, "Are you cold?" However, we realized he had put his foot in his mouth when everyone gasped and burst into laughter.

Our hostess graciously explained to Dave that what he had just asked Claudia was not, "Are you cold?" but, "Are you sexually frigid?" What he should have said was, "Is it cold to you?"

Have you ever thought you were saying the correct words, but communicated a totally different message? Sometimes in trying to show love to each other, we may communicate the opposite of what we want to say. At times, it's like we are speaking two different languages—and we may be! Especially if we don't understand the different languages of love.

Just as the whole world doesn't speak English, we can't assume that our mate will always understand our words and what we mean. We may not realize that we actually have different love languages, and of those languages there are many different dialects—as many as there are different personalities.

Understanding and accepting our mate's unique personality is a prerequisite to understanding our languages of love. Most people are capable of speaking more than one language of love, but their mother tongue is the predominant way they want to be loved. To keep your marriage growing, it's important to identify your love languages. At times, you may need to translate your partner's love language into your mother tongue. Like our garden-party experience, word-for-word translations don't always work. You need to look for the cultural equivalent!

What Is a Love Language?

Here's our definition: A love language is any way you let your spouse know you really care and understand how he or she feels, and that you respect those feelings. Anyone can handle stress easier if he knows there is just one other person who understands and cares. So take the time to learn to speak your mate's language of love.

Following are several of our love languages. See if you can identify with us.

Practical love. One of the most loving things Dave ever did for Claudia was to buy a copier for our home office. Before that, Claudia was continually running to the quick-print shop to make copies. So each time she looks at that copier, she knows how practical Dave's love is!

Romantic love. Dave is usually the romantic in our relationship. If Claudia wants to speak his language, she lights the lantern Dave gave her for her birthday to let him know she wants to speak romantically.

Self-sacrificing love. The key to understanding and speaking this love language is to be other-centered rather than self-centered. One of the most loving things Dave does is to take walks with Claudia to help keep her back healthy and strong.

Affirming love. Claudia needs a lot of feedback. Dave knows this, and when Claudia is writing an article, he willingly listens to Claudia's fifteen different edits of the same page! Affirming love can be expressed in letters, notes, telephone messages, hugs, and kisses.

Task-oriented love. This love is a first cousin to practical love, but it is expressed by completing a specific task. For example, one of the most loving things Claudia can do for Dave is to clean off her desk, which faces his desk. When her vertical files slip over onto Dave's side, it's time to speak task-oriented love—quick!

Bonding love. One of the most loving things either of us can do for the other is to plan some time alone. Think about those situations that pull you together, and help you bond.

What's Your Love Language?

Reflect on your own marriage. What are your favorite love languages? What are your mate's favorites? For the next few days, concentrate on loving your mate in his or her special language. And whatever your languages, use them all to say, "I love you!"

Chapter 27

Mission of a Marriage

We sat across the table, catching our breath, as Collin and Ruth shared with us about their busy lives. Missionaries to Africa, they were in the States on home leave for the summer with their four children, who ranged from preschoolers to teenagers! Most of the conversation centered on their children and their work in Africa. We then asked them how their marriage was going.

Married for twenty-two years, Collin and Ruth have a solid relationship. But both were speechless when Claudia popped the big question: "What are you looking forward to about the empty nest—you know, the half of your marriage that will be left when the kids are gone?"

After a few moments of silence, Ruth answered, "I've never thought about it! I just want to get through today!"

What would you answer? What are your plans for your marriage when your kids grow up and leave home? If you don't think about it now and set goals for your marriage, other things will take priority and your marriage will get what is left over at the end of the day.

We remember fantasizing about all the time we would have for each other when the kids grew up and left home. Looking back, we see this was overly optimistic. When there were no more soccer games, school lunches, or car pools, a legion of time-grabbers took their place. Our lives simply accelerated when our kids left home. We have to work just as hard—sometimes harder—to stay focused on our marriage. But it helps to have a marriage mission statement.

Businesses and organizations invest immense amounts of time to come up with a mission statement—the essence of what they want to be and accomplish. Shouldn't we do at least as much in our marriages? We've discovered that we invest more in our marriage when we work toward fulfilling our marriage mission statement. Our challenge to you is to take time right now to reflect on where you are in your marriage and where you would like your marriage to be when your nest is empty. Will that other bird in your nest be your best friend when the baby birds leave? Will you fly together in two-part harmony? We hope so. There's hope you can make it happen—if you take time now to dream together, set goals as a couple, and put them in your own mission statement for your marriage.

You can make it as simple or elaborate as you want, but your statement should express your deep desires for your marriage. In our Marriage Alive Seminar, couples write their mission statement for their marriage as a contract of what they both want to see happen. The shortest Marriage Mission Statement we've seen was three words, "Survive and abide!"

One couple wanting to emphasize commitment to their marriage relationship wrote their Marriage Mission Statement as an acrostic using the word *commitment*:

Creative use of conflict for marital growth

Openness in our communication

Maintain awareness of the state of our relationship

Mount full-scale war against outside attacks on our marriage

Intentionally apply marriage-building skills we've learned

Teamwork is vital—we both have valuable input
Model for our children and others the teachings of Christ
Encourage each other each day
Nurture each other, spiritually, physically, emotionally
Trust one another

As you write out your Marriage Mission Statement, take plenty of time and work together until you are both satisfied with the wording and content. But then remember that your statement is somewhat fluid—keep looking for better ways to express your desires for your marriage. We keep revising and editing ours. At our last edit, here is where we hope our marriage is heading.

Our Marriage Mission Statement

As a couple, we are committed to the pursuit of the following goals for our marriage partnership:

- A commitment to growth by regularly setting goals and objectives for our marriage.
- A commitment to communicate our true feelings, to build up and encourage each other, and to process and work through anger and conflict situations.
- A commitment to find space in our togetherness and unity in our diversity and to continue to grow as individuals.
- A commitment to strive to model for our own children and for others the outworking of the teachings of Christ about creative love in close relationships.
- A commitment to laugh, love, and have fun together.

Once you have completed your Marriage Mission Statement, take the first step in making it a reality. Remember, a long journey begins with the first step. Look at your mission statement and choose one area to start. List several practical steps you can take right now, then take one!

For us, we're putting down our writing and going out for a walk together.

Chapter 28

"It'll Only Take Ten Minutes"

There's a saying in the Arp family that creates all kinds of apprehension. Even Dave, who is not time-oriented, knows that when he hears Claudia utter this phrase, he needs to clear his calendar for the rest of the day.

It all started years ago when we made a major move. We were getting settled, which meant wallpapering the whole place. Over the years, whenever we moved, we always tried to get our boys' rooms settled first. We were in the process of doing just that when our friends, Clark and Ann, came for a visit. Claudia timidly asked, "Would you like to help us wallpaper one wall in Jonathan's room? It'll only take ten minutes."

Hours later, covered with wallpaper paste, Clark and Ann had learned the true meaning of the phrase, "It'll only take ten minutes!" Twenty years later, whenever we visit them, they still laugh about the "ten-minute" wallpapering job.

"It'll only take ten minutes" became an Arp motto. No matter what needed to be done, ten minutes should do it!

When our three sons were approaching their adolescent years, we decided we needed a place where we could retreat for a few moments of calm. As we surveyed our home, the logical location for such a spot was, of course, our bedroom.

So when Dave heard the words, "It'll only take ten minutes!" he knew he'd been had. Rearranging furniture is not one of his favorite activities—and he has the bad back to prove it. But he agreed to go along with Claudia's plans for the bedroom makeover.

Claudia had it all planned. All that was needed was Dave's muscle and patience. On this day he had little of either one. He was doing okay until Claudia said, "Hmm . . . I believe the bed would look better on that other wall after all." The ten allotted minutes stretched into longer than we care to mention.

Do you find yourself in those situations when your time is gobbled up by something that should only take ten minutes? Building a marriage and building a family are both time-intensive tasks. The problem is that time for both is elusive. Family needs usually demand attention, while time for marriage building is often an unfulfilled wish. How can we find a little time for our partner?

Start With Ten Minutes

If you want to start working on your marriage, couldn't you begin with just ten minutes? There really are some things you can do in a ten-minute time slot. Consider the following fifteen possibilities:

1. Make a list of things you would like to do together to build your marriage.
2. Sit down together for a cup of coffee or a glass of iced tea.
3. Talk about a chapter of this book that you've both read.
4. Take a walk around the block.
5. Read a short passage of Scripture and pray together.
6. Clean the bathroom together.
7. Exercise together.
8. Pop popcorn together and eat it!
9. Go into your bedroom closet, shut the door, and hug and

kiss until the kids find you.

10. Take a shower together and wash each other's hair.
11. Turn off the lights and sit alone in the dark together and neck.
12. Plant a flower together.
13. Write a letter of appreciation to your mate.
14. Together fold the basket of clean clothes and put them away.
15. Tell your kids how fortunate they are to have parents who love each other!

Let us encourage you to find ten minutes each day when you can concentrate on each other. Think about it. You'll still have twenty-three hours and fifty minutes left for all the other things you need to do—like wallpapering and rearranging furniture!

Chapter 29

Computers, E-mail, and Other Things That Should Work

We stared at the screen. The e-mail message we had just received from our son, Jarrett, had been replaced in an instant by those words every computer owner hates to have flash up on the screen: "system error." When we tried to correct it, things were worse; the screen was completely blank. Our almost-instant communication with our son flip-flopped into total isolation.

Dave's response? "It should have worked."

The problem with computers is words like "should", "assume", and of course there's always the sentence, "No, I don't have the backup disk." If computers and e-mail always worked as they *should*, they *would* be delightful. Unfortunately, we find them delightfully frustrating. It's so great when they work and so terrible when they don't!

Here's how we got into this mess. We're always eager to stay in touch with our sons, who are now grown and starting families of their own. So when one of our sons said, "Mom, Dad, you have to get an e-mail address so we can all communicate with each other even though we live far apart," we were interested. But it took relocating to Vienna, Austria for a temporary job assignment to push us over the edge and into the twenty-first century of surfing the Internet. The first thing we learned was that "It should work!" doesn't always mean it does!

While getting our e-mail address set up and learning the basics was a little frustrating, it did have its rewards—like the first e-mail message we got from family! And then the thrill of reading on our own personal e-mail that our next grandchild was going to be a boy! Everything was working out just dandy—until the computer screen flashed "system error."

Isn't that like life? Just as we think we have things all under control, something happens that shouldn't. Or we assume something will work, but it doesn't. Or our "backup" energy and stamina just aren't there. Our resources for handling the "errors" of life are limited. When we think wisely, this leads us to our Heavenly Father who never disconnects from us! God is the only constant energy source—when our resources run out, His are just beginning! We can be "off-line" with our family and friends, but never with God.

As we stared at our blank screen, somehow He heard our feeble cry for help. After a couple of hours of Dave "playing" with our laptop computer, access to our e-mail suddenly reappeared. Here was renewed hope in a hopeless situation! We were back on-line—just in time to get the request from one of our sons for financial aid!

Are we glad we moved into the twenty-first century and became e-mailers? You bet! Along with the frustrations are some great benefits of communicating across the miles!

Here are some of the discoveries we've made about how e-mail can revolutionize your family communication:

- It cuts down on miscommunication when everyone receives the same message.
- It omits the nonverbal language and tone of voice.

Receivers only need deal with the words, so it is easier to really "hear" the person sending the message.

- The quiet members of the family can easily participate.
- It's fast and easy—when it works as it *should*!
- For busy parents, it's a great way to stay in touch during the day.
- For the business traveler, it's the next best thing to a phone call.
- It's relatively inexpensive.
- It keeps you humble and teaches patience when the screen says "system error!"

Electronic mail confirms that you can teach old dogs new tricks—it just might take some of us longer! Recently we were visiting a dear friend who, at age ninety-three, still learns faster than any "dog" we know! She keeps a running list of questions for her granddaughter and granddaughter's husband for her weekly chat with them. At the top of her list, we noticed she had written "What's e-mail?" She could have asked us. Now we know!

Chapter 30

How Do I Love Thee?

A favorite song from our dating days is "Love Is a Many-Splendored Thing." It described the energy, enthusiasm, and excitement of our growing love for each other.

Perhaps you also remember the thrills of young love—of your dating days and the honeymoon years of your marriage. But over time, things begin to settle down. You discovered the person you thought was just about perfect also has some irritating habits. She's a blanket hog. He hums when he sleeps. Like us, did those early stars in your eyes fade enough that you started to see the other's idiosyncrasies? While love is still "a many-splendored thing," the realities of living together create tension that can cloud the skies of romantic bliss.

Life becomes even more complicated when the marriage duo expands to three, four, five, or more. However many children you have, the psalmist reminds us that children are a heritage from the Lord (Ps. 127:3). While we agree with the psalmist, we've also found that children are a very hectic heritage who bring out the best and the worst in us.

The Best, The Worst

As our children grew, our selfishness would surface when we'd say, "It's your turn to change the diaper . . . find the pacifier . . . settle the brothers' squabble. I want a little peace and quiet!"

But our children also revealed our best when we chose to have a servant's heart and volunteered for nighttime ear infection duty, or offered to drive the car-pool brigade who were impatiently honking to leave for basketball practice, or folded the laundry and put in the next load of clothes while remembering to clean the lint filter.

It's the day-to-day family living that provides the backdrop for loving each other with God's love. His love is a self-sacrificing love. His love is the kind of love that seeks to serve, rather than be served. It's the love that Jesus modeled and it's absolutely necessary if you want your love to be a many-splendored thing. True love is an attitude of caring more for that other person than you care for yourself. And love is expressed in little acts of kindness.

Love Is . . .

We asked the readers of our column in *Christian Parenting Today* magazine and participants in our Marriage Alive Seminars to share how they demonstrated servant love to each other. We were impressed with how many were able to take irritating situations and turn them into gifts of love. It is proof that true love can reside with reality. Here are several of those definitions of true love:

- Love is holding hands when one of you is discouraged and not saying, "I told you so."
- Love is exercising together after the holidays.
- Love is saying, "Go back to sleep, honey. I'll get the baby."
- Love is cleaning out the walk-in closet so you can walk in.
- Love is going to the neighborhood drugstore and buying a pregnancy test.

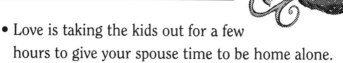

- Love is taking the kids out for a few hours to give your spouse time to be home alone.
- Love is turning your socks right side out before throwing them into the clothes hamper.
- Love is taking the kids to work for a day giving the stay-at-home parent a day off.
- Love is waiting patiently on hold when interrupted by call waiting.
- Love is taking the four pairs of shoes from the TV room back to the bedroom.
- Love is volunteering together at a soup kitchen.
- Love is going shopping together when you'd rather do anything else.
- Love is folding your spouse's towel and putting it back on the rack.
- Love is cleaning the tub for her when your wife is too pregnant to bend over.
- Love is sharing the best and worst of your day.
- Love is praying together.

To this list we could add, "Love is not always easy. Sometimes it is way beyond hard." This letter from a reader of our column shows how hard love can be—but also what we can learn from it:

"My husband's father passed away recently. I had to make many sacrifices for him and his family. I needed my husband with me and the children, but the Lord gave me patience and strength. Through this experience, I learned what it means to deny myself and serve others unrelentingly and with joy."

This is one mom who reminds us that true servant love really is a many-splendored thing!

Chapter 31

The Marriage Supper Club

One thing we always agree on—we like to eat! But we didn't realize how eating could enrich our marriage until we joined an "Ultimate Supper Club."

You might be thinking: *What in the world is that?* Well, it's an opportunity to combine good food and good times while enriching your own marriage and encouraging other couples to do the same!

If you're like us, you have more demands on your time than time itself. We've found that when we are under stress and pressure, the two things that tend to go are fun with friends and fun times with each other. We're not alone. According to a recent survey of couples who have attended our Marriage Alive Seminars, the top two unmet needs of most married couples are more time for fun and a desire to build a marriage partnership. We've discovered that an Ultimate Supper Club can help meet both of these needs!

What Is a Supper Club?

An Ultimate Supper Club can be whatever you want it to be. For us it means getting together monthly with several other couples who are also committed to helping their marriages grow. We know how important it is in our own marriage to have supportive and encouraging couple friendships. Our friends are there for us in the hard times, and at other times we enjoy each other's successes. In our supper club, we like to paraphrase Ecclesiastes 4:9,10—verses we often claim for our marriage—and apply them to our couple friends:

"Two or more couples are better than one, because they have a good return for their work: If one couple falls down, their couple friends can help them up. But pity the couple who falls and has no one to help them up!"

In today's world, where divorce is so common, we can all benefit from supportive couple friends who can help us up when we fall down.

How Do You Start a Club?

If you don't have supportive friendships with other couples right now, you can start to develop them. You can start an Ultimate Supper Club! All you need are a few couples (three other couples is ideal) and four evenings in the next four months. We've discovered that other couples are willing to participate if the club has a beginning and end and is not a permanent commitment. Take turns getting together once a month in each others' homes. Each meal can be a potluck dinner where everyone contributes, or the host couple can prepare the meal for the other couples. We like the latter option—you get three dinners out by preparing just one for the group!

While the cuisine may be appealing, the unique thing about the Ultimate Supper Club is that it is also good for your health—your marital health! While enjoying the food, fun, and fellowship, you'll have the opportunity to focus on your marriage, with a unique blend of fun and purpose.

You can create your own agenda and fun for your club. Choose a theme for each dinner party with conversation-starters and enhancers based on the evening's topic. For example, you may want to make the emphasis of the first evening together, "Making Our Marriage a High Priority." The couples can bring their wedding photos and share stories of how they met.

After dinner in our club, we have a short, practical Bible study. The first time you meet, you might explore Genesis 2:24 and discuss what it means today to "leave, cleave, and become one flesh."

To continue the fun, challenge the couples to have a date with their mates before the next time you meet. Share creative dating suggestions with each other. This will help you get out of the rut of dinner and a movie out!

Why Should We Go to All This Trouble?

An Ultimate Supper Club will help you focus on your own marriage relationship while encouraging your friends to do the same. Besides, it's just plain fun! If you're convinced, now's the time to get started. Make a list of potential couples to invite and plan a time to get together to talk about it—perhaps over coffee, tea, and a light dessert. Trust us, it's programmed for success. Everyone likes to talk and eat!

To whet your appetite, we're including some of the Arp family's favorite Supper Club menus! Enjoy!*

ITALIAN EXTRAVAGANZA
Homemade Pizza and Bruchette
Linguine with White Clam Sauce
Caesar Salad
Biscotti (Italian cookies—Yum!)

EASY FEAST

Raw Vegetables & Dip
Honey-baked Ham
Potato Salad (from your favorite deli)
Corn on the Cob
Green Beans
Rolls
Ice Cream

TRY VEGETARIAN

Roquefort Quiche
Fruit Salad
Whole Wheat Bread
Vegetable Medley
Chocolates & Coffee

NEVER ENOUGH ITALIAN

Minestrone Soup
Manicotti
Garlic Bread
Gelato

*Menus taken from *The Ultimate Marriage Builder*. For a Bible study
and guide for the Ultimate Supper Club see our book, *The Ultimate Marriage
Builder* (Nashville: Thomas Nelson, 1994), 223.

Chapter 32

In Sickness

The honeymoon suite was romantic, complete with heart-shaped spa and a dozen red roses. Definitely a great setting for a twentieth-anniversary celebration. But not this time! We grabbed our roses, took one last glance at the untouched room just waiting for us to enjoy it, and started the hour-long drive home to our youngest son who was sick and needed us.

Later that evening, as we spent a quiet twentieth anniversary with Jonathan, we remembered the phrase from our wedding liturgy: "in sickness and in health." We decided it should also include, "and in your children's illnesses, too."

We don't know about your kids, but ours seemed to have a radar that signaled, "Mom and Dad have plans—it's time to get sick!" Other traumatic memories include our three year old falling off a jungle gym and biting through his lip. We'll never forget racing to the hospital with another son who ran into a barbed-wire fence while playing soccer.

At other times, our own sicknesses have ruined great getaway plans. Nothing zaps a romantic occasion like getting ill. On a trip out west to record radio programs for The Family Workshop, it seemed logical to piggyback a visit to one of our favorite romantic spots in the Oregon mountains. But we discovered that the ideal time for a marriage getaway isn't immediately after recording sixty-eight high-energy marriage and family enrichment programs.

Tired and emotionally exhausted, we arrived in Oregon.

Romantic? You've got to be kidding! By the time we got to our secluded hideaway, Dave had bronchitis and couldn't lie down without having a coughing attack. He slept on the couch in the living room so that exhausted Claudia could get a little uninterrupted rest in the bedroom. This was definitely not the ultimate marriage builder.

We usually find the grace to love each other and handle the big disappointments that come along, like our bronchitis-bombed romantic getaway or our children's traumatic illnesses and injuries. There's a special closeness that comes from facing crises together. But what about the little chronic situations that just won't go away, like allergies, migraine headaches, PMS, or daily fatigue? Sometimes it's the little things that zap our energy and patience.

In today's fast-paced world, it's pretty easy to get rundown. And should the flu bug bite, how can we better love each other in sickness as well as in health? There's the obvious—get plenty of rest, exercise, and eat well. But you might also try these strategies, which we've found to be helpful when sickness or other crises strike:

- Pace yourself. Life is a marathon, not a sprint. Learn when to say no and save your strength. This may not be the year to give all the relatives homemade birthday gifts.
- Focus on the eternal, not the urgent. For the next month, read one chapter of Proverbs each day and pray with your spouse. Keep a prayer list and commit all your cares to the Lord.
- Take time to talk. Reserve ten minutes each morning or evening when you simply share how you feel—whether you're up, down, or somewhere in between.
- Give your mate a sincere compliment each day.

- Choose only one short-term goal at a time, like organizing your desk, kitchen, or closet.

And if sickness comes anyway? Take our prescription:

- Give yourself permission to do nothing. Try to let other family members carry the load.
- While bedridden, do some guilt-free sleeping, reading, or listening to your favorite music.
- If you're the caregiver, give your patient a "sick bell." He or she will feel some much-needed TLC when, at one ring, you come running.
- Make "pamper pills" by writing sweet nothings on slips of paper. Fold and put them in a jar to be drawn at leisure. You may need to stick around if you include something like, "I'll scratch your back!"
- Remember, this is temporary. Life will return to normal.

Take it from us. As we sit here by the fire on a cool evening, we barely remember Dave's hacking Oregon cough. While it's much more enjoyable to love in health than in sickness, both are vital if you want to have a growing, healthy marriage.

Chapter 33

Footprints to Follow

Our grandson, Walker, isn't walking yet. But when he does, his feet will be warm and toasty like the rest of the Arp clan! We just sent him his first pair of Austrian *Hutten Schuhe*. Now Walker is a real Arp!

Our family—with sons, daughters-in-law, and grandchildren—now numbers eleven, and we all have something in common. On any given cold morning, all around the world, you'll find the Arp clan keeping their feet warm with Austrian bedroom slippers. The only difference is the size and the color. The Austrian name for our house shoes is quite appropriate since this Arp tradition was born in a little Austrian hut.

Many of our favorite family traditions have just happened. The Austrian bedroom-slipper tradition is one we just . . . well . . . sort of slipped into! It started years ago when we lived in Austria and were planning a Christmas family vacation. Instead of multiple gifts for Christmas, we decided to give our boys and ourselves a few days of skiing. But our limited budget forced us to bring out our creativity.

We found an old isolated hunter's cabin nestled in the Austrian Alps. And we really mean isolated! It was just us, the Alps, and snow—no television, radios blaring, or traffic racing by. Just the creative noises of three boys sledding down the virgin snow-covered hills and trying to avoid snowballs coming from all directions! About a mile down the path was a small family ski lift—just right for a family with three little boys. And did we mention cheap?

The cabin was simple. We're talking basic and rustic! We did have running water and electricity, but that was about it. Each room had a ceramic woodburning stove—and the wood was behind the cabin just waiting to be cut!

Brrrrr!

When we arrived, a snowdrift covered more than half the front door. We found it waiting for us after we had forged a path up the hill to get to the door. We were eager to build a toasty fire to warm up, and that's where our bedroom-slipper tradition began.

The week before our ski trip, Claudia discovered these house shoes at a quaint little shoe shop. Anticipating the primitive condition of our ski cabin, and looking for a fun yet practical gift, she bought *Hutten Schuhe* for all five Arps. These unique slippers are made for such an occasion. The bottom is soft leather, but the slipper is lined in wool and the upper part of the shoe is boiled wool. Boiling shrinks the wool and makes it extra thick and warm. Just what we needed! So as we sat by the stove, wearing our new slippers, our feet were toasty warm.

The slippers were so nifty that we continued to wear them. Over the years, as the slippers wore out (or little feet grew out of them), we replaced them with new ones. Even after our sons grew up and left home, whenever we would get together, there were the slippers! As daughters-in-law joined our family, they were initiated into our slipper tradition. The slippers even gave us the clue we needed to realize that our youngest son, Jonathan, and his girlfriend Autumn's relationship was becoming more serious. One day, he asked us to pick up slippers for

Autumn. She is now our third daughter-in-law. Even our grandchildren have their own pairs of Austrian bedroom slippers.

Family Traditions

What are your favorite family traditions? Some you may have planned, but are there some, like our slipper tradition, that just happened? Are you doing anything that perhaps is becoming a tradition, but you're not yet aware of it? Are there some things you enjoy doing that could be adopted as a long-term tradition? one dad we know started the tradition of making pancakes for his family every Sunday night. This tradition started when the second child was born and Mom desperately needed help! Now it's a weekly family-time tradition no one wants to miss.

Family traditions and habits give a rhythm to life. There's a sense of security in being able to say, "We always do it this way in our family." Traditions pull us together when outside forces threaten to push us apart. Traditions give us a sense of unity and encouragement in the hard times. Traditions are precious gifts we can pass on to future generations.

Marriage Traditions

What about your marriage? What healthy traditions are you modeling and passing on to future generations? Consider the following traditions that are easy to start and are wonderful marriage enhancers to pass on:

- Always kissing when you say good-bye.
- Always kissing when you say hello.
- Having a weekly or monthly "date night."
- Praying together before you go to sleep at night.
- Making apple-walnut pancakes on Saturday morning.

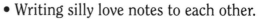

• Writing silly love notes to each other.

• Feeding the birds together.

You might want to make a list of traditions you already have. Then make a list of those you would like to start and look for new ideas and opportunities. It's amazing what happens in a relationship when you're living in anticipation of discovering new ways to enjoy each other.

Years later, after our Christmas vacation and the initiation of our Arp slipper tradition, we were back in Austria where one of our sons was being married. Guess what they gave as gifts to their wedding attendants? Austrian bedroom slippers, of course! They were married in January in a very cold, beautiful little Austrian church. And during their wedding ceremony they wore . . . Austrian bedroom slippers!

Our challenge to you is to take the ordinary and make it special. Capture memories. Build traditions. Pass them on to future generations. Then you will be leaving footprints to follow!

Chapter 34

In the Bank!

"If we only had more hours in our day and more bucks in the bank, we could balance our lives," complained Sarah, a young mother of three preschoolers. Sarah, a work-at-home mom, isn't alone in her frustration. We all could use more time and money.

Trust us, the time and money shortages don't end when your children grow up! Through the years, the two areas of greatest tension in most marriages are financial and time pressures. Often, these even seem to be linked to each other. As you set financial goals and work hard together to achieve them, it's possible to end up with things you want to have, but no time to enjoy them! We can become slaves to our possessions. We can seem to have it all, but actually have nothing.

M. Scott Peck, author of *The Road Less Traveled*, points out that one sign of maturity is the ability to delay gratification. We live in an instant world—instant oatmeal, instant coffee, and instant credit. Lately, we've noticed how many "pre-approved" credit-card offers we get in the mail. When our sons were in college and didn't have two pennies to rub together, they regularly got offers for credit cards with spending limits that could break a small bank!

The temptation to assume debt and overspend is prevalent everywhere! We're told we can have it all and have it right now.

If you're bored and have the right credit card, you can whisk your mate off to a romantic island—no need to get baby-sitters or even pack. We are told to "Just do it!" But we wonder: If that phrase were switched to "Just wait until you have the resources," how many problems in marriage would be lessened?

We're certainly not financial wizards or time-management experts. We don't have it all together in these areas, but we do work on them! Perhaps, though, we could all benefit from a few tips:

- While no one likes to talk about the "B" word, budgets can be excellent marriage enrichers! If you don't have one that works, we suggest finding a good book on finances. If you use a computer, check with your local computer store for the latest software that's designed to help you with your finances and investments. (Two helpful tools are "Quicken" and "Manage Your Money.")

- From time to time, we write down everything we spend. When we record every expenditure, we notice a marked difference in our attitude toward spending. It's easy to evaluate where our money goes and to make necessary changes. When we did this recently, we realized that we needed to eat more meals at home—which meant cutting back on time commitments so we would have more time to prepare homemade meals.

- We also try to limit our credit-card spending to what we can pay off each month. When things are really tight, we try not to use credit cards. Suzy and Hank, parents of three girls who all like to shop, came up with their own recipe for handling plastic: Preheat oven to 400 degrees F, and bake the cards for ten minutes!

- We try to save. How much isn't as critical as developing the habit. You may want to choose
  long-term goals like retirement and your children's educa-
  tion. Or a short-term goal might be starting a fund for a
  twenty-four-hour getaway for two! Consider choosing a
  family goal. For example, you might have a family garage
  sale to help finance a family vacation. Our sons (with help
  from Mom) made and sold wax Christmas-tree decorations
  to help finance family-fun activities.
- We try to experience the joy of giving. One Christmas we
  bought presents for all the children in a family experiencing
  financial distress. Today, our most precious memory of that
  Christmas is what we gave—no one remembers what we got!
  Is there a family you could help? And while we're talking
  about the holidays and giving, what gifts could you give each
  other this year that money can't buy? Coupons for time
  alone, kitchen cleanups, baby sitting, and surprise dates are
  all marriage enrichers. Consider giving your spouse (and
  each child) a coupon for an hour alone with you.

A noted psychologist said one key to successful parenting is
to spend half as much money on your kids and twice as much
time. The key to a growing, living marriage is to spend half as
much money on things and twice as much time with your
spouse!

Chapter 35

Realizing Our Roles

As we avoided another biker on a heavily traveled, narrow mountain road, Claudia said, "Thank you for driving!"

"You're welcome," Dave replied, wondering what motivated Claudia to be so grateful.

Whenever we travel, Dave is the driver. We never planned it that way, but it has become his role—chief driver and traffic- and bike-dodger. Without realizing it, we do have roles in our marriage.

Some say roles in marriage are passé, but we disagree. We do agree that some of the old forms of marriage don't work, but roles will be with us forever. Some roles we choose and others just appear over time.

For instance, we do have our traveling roles. But before we became conscious of these roles, Claudia felt a little put-upon each time we prepared to leave on another trip. She is the expert family packer, and has an uncanny way of knowing just what and how much we need to take so we don't run out of clothes or have to wear our underwear inside out.

Actually, it was a great day when Claudia thanked Dave for driving. A little light had suddenly clicked on inside her head: "I pack, Dave drives—and those are our traveling roles!"

If one of us had to both drive and pack, something would be out of balance. Or if we said, "Dave, you're the man, so you have to drive!" and "Claudia, it's woman's work to pack," we'd lose the joy of serving each other. It's when we freely choose our roles that our marriage is blessed.

Much is written today about achieving reciprocity in marriage—the "I'll scratch your back if you'll scratch mine" philosophy. The problem is that in marriage, it just doesn't work. Fifty-fifty isn't good enough. Our good friend, Linda Dillow, says that in a healthy, happy marriage, the split must be 100/100. Each person has to give everything. We agree with her!

Two-Part Harmony

An enriched marriage can be compared to two different musical instruments playing different parts of the same song in harmony, each giving 100 percent to create beautiful music together. But where to invest your 100 percent depends on the roles you choose. For example, in our work as family-life educators, we work so closely together that sometimes it's hard to see where one's part ends or the other's begins. When we write together, we both have editorial say-so—often we don't remember who wrote what. We've learned one critical thing: there is no room for competition in our marriage. Competing is the opposite of harmonizing. If we're playing in harmony, it means we mutually respect each other and our unique gifts.

When marriage partners are comfortable with their roles, they respect each other. It's easy to see they are on the same team. You don't hear them putting each other down. They have a foundation of mutual respect. They are courteous and kind to one another. Their home has an atmosphere of love and acceptance. No battleground there! They play their roles in harmony and it's obvious they are united in their diversity.

Much has been written about headship and submission in

marriage, but very little about the admonition to submit to one another. As Christians, we are to think of others first. This is the simple, underlying foundation of mutual respect. Philippians 2:3 says it this way: "Do nothing out of selfish ambition or vain conceit, but in humility consider others better than yourselves." This meaning is simple: We are to put our mate's needs and desires before our own.

How are you doing at putting your mate first? Have you talked about your roles? Do you play together in harmony?

Take a few minutes and talk about how you see your marriage roles. Are you each giving 100 percent? Are there some roles you feel uncomfortable with? Are there areas where you have disagreement? Do you need to make some mid-course adjustments? Is there some way you can compromise?

Whatever your chosen roles, give your 100 percent. As you make lovely music together, you will have an enriched marriage—whether you do the driving or pack the bags!

Chapter 36

Label Us Tolerant!

Labels. We all use them. Are they positive or negative? It depends on who is doing the labeling and who is being labeled.

About a year ago, while we were on assignment with the United Nations' International Year of the Family, we experienced labeling from both sides. For us, it was a quick course in Tolerance 101. Perhaps from the nature of our assignment, you have already labeled us. Wait! There's more to the story.

When God opens a door, we must be faithful to walk through it. So when we had the opportunity to write one of the Occasional Papers for the International Year of the Family on the topic of family enrichment, we pursued it. We believed that God could close that door at any moment if He didn't want us there. But, He didn't! He just kept opening more, which even led to a three-month assignment in Vienna, Austria, speaking, starting parenting groups, and researching what families are doing right around the world. We've found you can't teach others without learning yourself. One of our biggest lessons was in tolerance.

Our chief contact at the United Nations was the Staff Counselor. His joy in life is helping people, and he delights in bringing people together who can connect and help others. He was the one who put us in contact with the leaders of the International Year of the Family. When he told us that someone had labeled us "very conservative," we were concerned that it might block doors of helping many families. Then we met Peter, who was very conservative himself. He labeled us "liberal."

What did we do? We simply labeled both "labelers" intolerant! Couldn't they understand our desire was simply to help families love one another just a little bit better? Why couldn't they both be more tolerant with us? Hmmmm. Maybe it was time for us to look in the mirror!

Have you ever noticed how intolerant tolerant people are of those less tolerant than they? And for us on that day, our mirror reflected "Guilty."

Intolerance isn't just an international liability. We find plenty of it in our own homes—in our families and marriages. And often the symptoms of intolerance in our homes are the labels we give each other: "He's messy." "She's a loner." "Johnny's a loudmouth." "Kelly is an underachiever." "My husband, George, is a pessimist." "Ruth, my wife, is disorganized." And, of course: "He/She just doesn't understand me!" In fact, we've noticed that many times misunderstanding is at the root of intolerance. And if we don't understand, we jump to conclusions.

For a marriage, intolerance is a real downer! So how can we label ourselves a little more tolerant? Tolerance starts in the home and with the individual.

Tolerance Begins with Understanding

We've already pointed out that the old adage, "opposites attract," was true in our experience. Our differences initially attracted us to each other. But after marriage, our differences weren't always easy to understand and led to misunderstandings and intolerance. Claudia's enthusiasm for life led to over-

commitment, and Dave's easygoing personality was sometimes misinterpreted as not caring.

Not only did we have difficulty tolerating each other, but
when we added three children—all with their different personalities—it became even harder!

Tolerance Is Forgiving and Accepting

We soon discovered that tolerance means forgiving and
accepting each other. We can't change the other person, but we
can change ourselves. An interesting thing happens when we
change. Others tend to change in response to us. When we're
having a hard time with each other, we make a list of what is
driving us crazy. Then we write out our inappropriate or intolerant reaction. That's what we have to deal with. Often that
involves asking the other's forgiveness for things we have said or
done. Then we must affirm that tolerance means respecting
other people being different!

Tolerance Is Concentrating on the Positive

As one dad told us, "I want to always protect my daughter's
'worth' nerve. I want her to feel good about who she is and I
want to affirm her in every way I can." Goethe, the great
German poet, said that if you treat a person as he is, he will stay
as he is. But if you treat that person as if he were the bigger and
better person he could be, he will become that bigger and better
person. Tolerance is looking at each other and our children
through Goethe's lens.

Tolerance Is Contagious

Tolerance begins in your family and reaches out to the
world. Tolerance starts with you and your love for your spouse

and children. In our paper for the International Year of the Family, we quoted Confucius, the Chinese philosopher, who is reputed to have said:

"When there is love in the marriage, there is harmony in the home; when there is harmony in the home, there is contentment in the community; when there is contentment in the community, there is prosperity in the nations; when there is prosperity in the nations, there is peace in the world."

The next time you don't understand your spouse and are ready to label him or her inconsiderate, uncaring, or unthoughtful, stop and think: Can you forgive, accept, and look for something—anything—that at that moment is positive? If so, we'd label your marriage a "growing marriage." And you earn the label "tolerant!"

Chapter 37

Choices

For miles ahead, all we could see was traffic. Not a single car or truck was moving! The Germans have a name for this travel phenomenon: It's called a *stau,* and it's not fun.

Perhaps you too have been stuck in traffic and you know the frustration we were feeling that particular day. What do you do?

You have two choices. You can wait it out. Or you can get off at the next exit and see what back roads you can find that will get you to your destination. One choice is boring. The other involves the unknown and requires you to take risks. Which would you take?

Marriage can be like the traffic jam on the main highway. We all face those times when our marriage relationship is stalled and boredom is threatening. Are you willing to take the risk to venture out on an unknown course? Or do you choose to play it safe and stay put—your relationship is uninteresting and boring, but you are together?

We often hear, "We've thought about coming to your Marriage Alive Seminar, but we don't want to mess with our marriage." What these couples are saying is, "It's safe here on the interstate. We're not willing to take the risk, even though we are at a standstill."

The Marriage Adventure

Building an enriched marriage should be a continual adventure. We asked Phil and Michelle, who have a fun and enriched marriage, what they hoped their children would remember from their home when they are adults. The answer made sense to us: "We'd like for our kids to say that they never knew what to expect!" That's not a bad goal for a marriage, either. After all, Marriage Enrichment is a first cousin to Family Enrichment. When you enrich your family, you enrich your marriage. And when you enrich your marriage, you also enrich your family. But what can you do to put some spice into your marriage and family life? What about trying something totally "off the wall"?

Our family still laughs about the time Claudia served popcorn for breakfast. Dave still hopes that one morning she'll break out the ice cream. Another family we know planned a backward meal—imagine the looks Mom got when she brought out the dessert first!

Perhaps you have a teenager who has a bad case of the blahs. Why not buy a package of balloons, blow them up, and write on each an encouraging note? Then stuff your teen's closet with them.

Why not add a little adventure to your marriage relationship? One day, Dave walked into our office and said, "Be ready at 7:00 P.M." That was all he said. As hard as Claudia tried, she couldn't get him to reveal what he had up his sleeve. But just knowing he had taken the initiative to plan something put an extra skip in her step. When seven o'clock came, still-curious Claudia eagerly got in the car. Where did we go? To the dollar movie! Even with popcorn and drinks, we had a fun adventure for under ten bucks!

Create Your Own Adventure

What can you do that is out of character or unexpected?

Check out these ideas from some creative
couples we know:

- Gene and Carol like to square-dance, and they recently
  learned how to do the Texas Two-Step.
- Ralph's a great golfer, but his wife, Meg, had never golfed.
  When she began golfing recently, they decided that when
  they golf together, they won't keep score.
- Judy and Mike are learning to speak Russian.
- Joe and Janice are taking a northern Italian cooking class.
- Ed and Maze pack up their backpacks and hike eleven
  miles each summer and stay in rustic quarters with no
  running water or electricity.
- Marlene and Steve, after twenty-five years of marriage, just
  attended their first marriage enrichment weekend.
- Kitty and Paul had a bookstore date and picked out a new
  book on building a creative love life.

Now it's your turn to take a risk—but don't worry, it's a cal-
culated risk and one that can bring great dividends. And the
next time you get caught in heavy traffic, work up your courage
and try a back road. You may not know exactly where you are,
but you can make it a great time together.

Chapter 38

You Gotta Have Heart!

As we walked into the restaurant, we were pleasantly surprised. On the table we had reserved for "The Arps" was a sign indicating that it was reserved for "The Hearts." This sounded considerably more romantic, and it put a love twist on the whole evening.

We all need "heart" in our marriage relationship! Somewhere between the dirty dishes in the sink, crusty half-eaten peanut-butter-and-jelly sandwiches, and blaring teenage music, it's easy to forget that "you gotta have heart!" What can we do to put a little romance back into our relationship?

Memory Lane

One place to "get some heart" is to think back to when you first met your sweetheart and first felt those romantic feelings stir. Do you remember the first time you saw your mate? We remember that day, but there were no romantic feelings. Dave was fifteen, Claudia was thirteen, and we remember it because Dave threw Claudia in the swimming pool with her clothes on! He didn't exactly make the right kind of splash in her life!

What about your first date? Can you remember where you went, how you felt? Our first date was a blind date and almost didn't happen. A mutual friend of our families encouraged Dave to ask Claudia out, but each time he called she was busy or out of town. Being the laid-back persistent type, he didn't give up. At last we connected. Claudia already had plans but she invited Dave along—to the youth group at Claudia's church, where she was speaking. Afterward we went to a movie.

What was your most romantic moment before you were married? We remember getting all dressed up and driving two hours to Atlanta, Georgia, going to a plush place for dinner and then dancing cheek-to-cheek. Claudia remembers that there on the dance floor, Dave said "I love you" for the first time! (Dave doesn't remember, but takes Claudia's word for it.)

What were some of your favorite dates before you were married? Maybe you could recreate some of them. One couple complained to us they had no money for dating. We asked them what they did before they were married. Their eyes lit up as they told us about having no money at all for dates, so they would make peanut butter sandwiches and take them to a park and eat them together. Guess what we suggested they do ASAP?

We remember going to Grassy Mountain. There was a wonderful lake. We hiked, talked, and hugged, and later Dave picked a leaf to go in our scrapbook so we would remember this day. To this day, there's no problem in remembering that special occasion. The leaf that he gave Claudia was a sprig of poison ivy! (You really don't want to know the rest of the story, but Claudia married him anyway!)

Your Own Lane

Let us encourage you to continue down memory lane. For a fun interlude after your kids are in bed, talk about the following memories:

- Do you remember the first time you ever talked about marriage?

- What do you remember most about your wedding day?
- What is your favorite memory about your honeymoon?
- Where was the first place you lived as husband and wife, and what was it like?
- Talk about the feelings you each had when your children were born.
- What times did you feel especially close to each other?
- What are some favorite memories you would recreate?

After you've enjoyed your trip down memory lane, make a "heart" list. Draw from your own memory bank and write down all those romantic times you would like to recreate.

We'll skip the fully clothed dip in the swimming pool. But we would like to go back to Grassy Mountain. When we get there, we'll hike, hug, and kiss. But this time we'll avoid the poison ivy!

Chapter 39

Take a Hike!

The crisp air and the leaves—just beginning to display their colors—made it a perfect day for a walk in the woods. Through the years, we've found walking to be a wonderful marriage enricher. Today, we were back in Austria where we lived when our boys were all growing up. With three active boys, we spent lots of time outdoors, so on this day family was on our minds.

"Dave," Claudia observed, "this is a wonderful walking path—it's level, smooth and delightful. Why didn't we find paths like this when we lived here?"

Dave's to-the-point answer: "We had kids!"

It's not that we didn't walk during those years, it's just that being young parents took us on different paths—paths that definitely required more energy, patience, and stamina!

Etched in our memory are the Boy Scout hikes. Each spring the Scouts invited parents to join them for a hike in the Vienna Woods. It was a challenging all-day hike and you had to make it up "Hell Hill" to finish the course and receive your *Wandertag Metal*. One year we missed the starting group and became hopelessly lost in the Vienna Woods with two seven year olds, five apples, and three hard-boiled eggs. (That was the day we were starting a diet.) It wasn't a fun walk!

We remember walking around every soccer field within a fifty-mile radius of Vienna, and walking down the black-diamond ski slopes that were too steep to maneuver, even though our sons told us we'd have no problems!

In those years we didn't always find smooth walking paths because we simply didn't have the time or energy. Now, in the afternoon of our marriage, we enjoy discovering paths more to our taste and pace. But we know we're enjoying this stage of our "marriage walk" because we hung in there during the hectic parenting years. And you can, too!

Walk, Don't Faint

Walking together through the parenting years goes better when we rely on God. Isaiah 40:29 says, "He gives strength to the weary and increases the power of the weak," and in the last part of verse 31, "they will walk and not be faint." (Isn't this every parent's goal?) In the midst of family life, you may feel faint and may not find time for long, leisurely strolls. But there are short walks you can take that will enrich your marriage and give you a break from the kids! Here are some of our favorites:

Walk for a cup of coffee. When we lived in Austria, we were within walking distance of a quaint little coffee shop. From time to time, we would slip away for a cup of cappuccino. If you don't live within walking distance of a coffee shop, drive and park your car several blocks away and walk.

Walk around soccer, football, and track fields. When you take your kids to practice, intentionally spend the hour walking around the track or local vicinity near the field. When practice is over, you'll feel refreshed and reconnected.

Walk around the church. Use the time while your children are at youth activities to capture a few moments alone with your spouse.

Walk to the corner market for bread and milk. When you

run errands, occasionally run them together. You'll find talking time you never knew existed.

Walk to your bedroom and close the door. When your kids hit their adolescent years, consider a bedroom makeover to create a comfortable sitting area for two. It can be your "getaway" if things get too crazy around the house. Find your own little corner and walk there often.

Walk to the kitchen when the dishes need doing. It's the one place most parents can go and be assured of being alone. Even if your kids' chores include kitchen cleanup, if you really want to talk in private, volunteer for KP.

Our Challenge to You

If you want to walk together in the afternoon of your marriage, when your children are grown and where the paths are delightfully smooth and enjoyable, take the time now for mini-walks with your mate.

Years later, you'll be glad you took the time to walk through life together with your partner. Trust us, you'll pass on an enriching, healthy tradition to your children and grandchildren.

Someday soon, we plan to take our granddaughter, Sophie, for a walk on the "Sophie Alp" in the middle of the Vienna Woods, where her father walked as a preschooler. And when our grandsons, Hayden and Walker, join us, who knows where the paths will lead!

Chapter 40

The Two-Career Seesaw

"Isn't it time somebody took out the garbage?" is more than a trite question. Divvying up household chores is a real issue for those parents—fifty-eight percent of all married couples—who walk a two-job tightrope.

Ed and Katie are among them. We met Ed and Katie at a Marriage Alive Seminar that was filled with two-career couples—and with frustrations evidenced by comments like Katie's: "What I need is thirty hours in each day. I could manage if only Ed would do his part. But when we get home in the evening, he checks out, and I'm left with the children and most of the chores!"

In spite of many unrealistic stereotypes—especially of "macho males" like Ed who don't get their hands wet—many parents pull together as they wrestle with jobs, kids, and busy schedules. It's not easy to balance the two-career seesaw, but it can get easier if you work with your working mate!

Assess Your Situation

To help Ed and Katie, we had them make a list of their individual responsibilities outside and inside the home, including their children's special needs. Then we asked them, "If you arranged all your various responsibilities on a seesaw, putting each person's responsibilities on opposite ends, how would your seesaw balance?"

For instance, if one mate works outside the home only part-time each week and the other regularly puts in a sixty-hour workweek, the at-home mate balances the seesaw by carrying more of the home load. Ed and Katie spent equal amounts of time and energy in their jobs outside the home, but their at-home list looked something like this:

Katie:

1. Prepare meals.
2. Grocery shop.
3. Do family laundry.
4. Keep the house clean.
5. Arrange for sitters.
6. Help children with homework.
7. Take children to youth activities at church.

Ed:

1. Take care of the yard.
2. Maintain cars.
3. Keep family financial records.

It was evident that Ed and Katie needed to make some adjustments. Ed's home responsibilities were important and took time, but he could accomplish them on weekends. Katie's responsibilities weren't so flexible—especially the children's needs—and demanded more of her than she could give after each workday.

Balance Your Seesaw

Sit down with your spouse and make your own list of responsibilities and see how your seesaw looks. Is one of you on "overload?" Does someone need to volunteer to take out the garbage or change the baby's diaper? It just may be you!

Next, make a list of all the household jobs and responsibilities that must be done. List everything you can think of from the obvious (like reading to the kids and putting them to bed at night, making beds, and cooking meals) to the less obvious (like cleaning closets, garage, and gutters, to doing the banking, caring for the pets, and planning family celebrations).

To divide responsibilities between you, identify the tasks you each like to do best and least. When we did this exercise, we went through our list from the perspective of which one of us could do the job better. (Claudia immediately conceded that Dave was the best bathroom cleaner in ten states.) In deciding who will do what, it's helpful to consider how often each task needs to be performed. Meal preparation is daily, but income tax returns are filed yearly.

Once Ed and Katie did this exercise, Ed became more aware of the stress Katie experienced as well as the need for his increased involvement at home. They discovered that the mechanics of who does what is not as important as the philosophy of working together as a team. They also recruited their children for jobs around the house, and for heavy jobs, they started hiring a cleaning service to come in once a month.

Ed and Katie's seesaw may still go up and down, but on most days it's much more balanced! How about yours? Isn't it time you changed the diapers or took out the garbage?

Chapter 41

How to Have a Love Life and Kids, Too!

We had just begun a session on building a creative love life in our Marriage Alive Seminar when a young mom spoke out of sheer frustration. She said, "With the children, extended family, jobs, church responsibilities, financial struggles, love life—I'm stuck in the fast lane with no way to slow down. Love life? What love life?"

As young parents, finding time for loving was hard for us, too. Dave was the night owl who eagerly looked forward to love-making after the baby's late-night feeding. Claudia, the morning lark, barely survived feeding the baby. All she wanted after that was sleep. Missing each other's expectations just made us grumpy in the morning. Claudia would have been up for loving at 5:00 A.M., but by then Dave was sawing logs and the baby was awake again.

Psychologists tell us that the two times of greatest stress on a marriage are when you have toddlers and when you have teens. The hardest time in our sexual relationship was when we had three children ages five and under. Sticky peanut butter and jelly on doorknobs, dirty dishes in the sink, and early Fisher-Price® decor didn't exactly set the mood for a loving rendezvous.

Maybe you find yourself in a similar situation. Children and the stresses of living drain your energy. Time for loving is elusive and rare. Maybe you aren't even sure if your mate cares.

You've thought about reading a book on how to salvage a run-down sex life, but you know you'd probably fall asleep before you finished the first chapter.

We survived those stressful years, and you can, too. You're okay. Your body works. Your children will grow up. And in the meantime, you can do several things to nurture your love life.

Remember, God is the originator of sexuality. He can empower you to build a creative love life in spite of the seemingly insurmountable obstacles. Too often, especially when children are young, other priorities take precedence over sex. At this stage of family life, your love life will have to be intentional and it may require some sacrifices.

Our friend, Jim, loves to golf. But with three children and one more on the way, he has decided that his Saturday games will just have to wait a few years. With the money and time he saves by not golfing each week, Jim and his wife, Abby, hire a sitter so they can be alone together.

We're not golfers, so we can't totally appreciate Jim's sacrifice, but Abby can. You may not have to give up golf, but you do have to make sacrificial choices to have a growing and creative love life. Here are some suggestions:

Find a weekly time when you can be alone without your children. You may think, "But that's just not spontaneous!" The fact is that spontaneity is not the guiding principle for having a creative love life during the parenting years. If you wait for spontaneity, your love life may spontaneously self-destruct!

Take the initiative. To a wife who bluntly asked us, "How can I make James want me?" we answered, "Let him know you're interested!" To some, this may seem too simplistic. Of course, human relationships are complex, and problems much deeper than sexual ones may block growth in any area, including the sexual one. If this is true in your experience, please get help from your pastor or a counselor. But for the average harried parents, there are some things you can do to attract your reluctant spouse. It takes one person to initiate. If you're the one who is interested—you're elected!

Choose to be creative. Deepening your marital bonds may require you to make yourself vulnerable by taking the initiative and choosing to be creative. Take the initiative to plan alone-times. Plan a night away to somewhere you've never been before. Do something surprising—this may help you break out of a rut. Romance is not exclusively reserved for the bedroom. You may want to try some of these ideas:

- Call to let your mate know you desire him or her.
- Write your mate a love letter.
- After the children are in bed, light some candles and put on some soft music.
- Spend at least one hour talking about loving each other.
- Give your mate an unexpected little gift.
- Tell your mate ten reasons why you love him or her.
- Buy a new "mood" music tape or CD.

Don't give up! Some things you try may bomb. Other things will work. When you're tired and discouraged, remember why you're doing this. Your goal is to build a creative love life that will last throughout the years of your marriage. Hang in there. Your children need to be reassured of your love for each other. Romance in the home is healthy and a great model for the next generation.

Someday your children may even facilitate your love life. One summer when our oldest son and his wife were going away for several weeks, they offered us their apartment in Williamsburg, Virginia for a getaway. We took them up on it.

Imagine our surprise when we found their table romantically set for two with candles and china.

We hope you'll continue to work on having an enriched love life in the midst of your hectic and harried world. You'll be enhancing your marriage and passing on a heritage of love to your children.

Chapter 42

Secrets of a Happy Marriage

Weddings always make us cry. This one was no exception. As the bride floated down the aisle on her father's arm, the eager groom gazed at her with complete love, affection, and anticipation. Nothing is more moving than attending a wedding and witnessing two people pledging their eternal love to each other. Yet, first marriages last an average of 6.3 years—considerably less than forever. Too often the "I do" dissolves into "I don't, I can't, and I won't." However, for every marriage that crumbles, another endures. What are some of the key ingredients in those good marriages that endure?

Some people think the keys for an enduring marriage are love and romance. While these are obvious and important prerequisites to launching a good marriage, they aren't enough to keep the marriage afloat.

More important than how much two people love each other, or how blissfully happy they are before their wedding day, is how well they talk and share and work out their problems after marriage. In other words, how they deal with their feelings matters more than what they're actually feeling.

But on this particular wedding day, problems and hard work were the last thing on the bride's and groom's minds. We know. During their engagement we gave them one of our books on marriage. We smiled at each other when they commented,

"We really like your book, *The Marriage Track*, but we won't need the chapter on 'Resolving Honest Conflict.' We're so in love that we'll never have problems." Silently we noted their first problem!

Sure enough, a year later they were fighting it out—both enrolled in an intensive informal course called Marriage 101! They were learning together how to work out the problems they never were going to have. Someone wisely said, "Marriage is an attempt to solve problems you wouldn't have if you had never become a couple."

Many couples do work hard and build enriched, happy marriages. What does a happy marriage look like? Here are ten characteristics of happy couples. Check and see how many describe your marriage!

1. They are best friends. They enjoy being together and have interests in common.
2. They listen to and confide in each other. They listen with their hearts as well as their ears, and they don't use what they hear to attack the other person.
3. They are tuned-in to each other's feelings. They say what they mean and mean what they say, but they never use manipulation to get their way.
4. They can deal with negative emotions. And when they share negative emotions, they accept responsibility for their own feelings. They generally start their sentences with "I" and let the statement reflect back on them. They seek feedback from their spouse.
5. They know how to handle conflict. They are committed to attacking problems, not each other. They look for solutions that both can live with. Compromise is not a dirty word!
6. They're less than brutally honest. In other words, they

think before they speak.

7. They trust each other. They feel totally safe in each other's presence and don't doubt their loyalty to each other.

8. They're committed to making the marriage work. Divorce is not an option and they don't even kid about it! They see their marriage relationship as a priority and take the time to make it work.

9. They share interests. While there is diversity in their unity, they look for interests they can share together—from walking, to sailing, to gourmet cooking. From time to time they adopt new hobbies they can do together.

10. They're flexible enough to change and tolerate change. They're willing to change to keep their marriage living and growing. They realize that different seasons of life bring new challenges to their marriage, and they accept those challenges willingly, knowing they will produce lasting growth.

The good news from the marriage researchers is that a couple learns how to be happily married. It's possible to master the skills needed to make your relationship better. Why not take time and go through this list with your spouse and choose an area to concentrate on? You, too, can personally experience the secrets of a happy marriage.*

*This chapter adapted from Dave and Claudia Arp, *60 One-Minute Marriage Builders* (Nashville: Thomas Nelson, 1993).

Chapter 43

John and Janie's Weekend Fix

Our friend, John, told us this story: "It's pretty common for me not to know what my wife, Janie, is going to do. But this time she really surprised me! Here's the story: It was Friday afternoon. She walked into my office at work and pulled out a blindfold. Everyone there knew what was going on except me. The next thing I knew, I was in the car, and she was telling me to relax, that she was kidnapping me for a getaway weekend."

"An hour and a half later she stopped the car and removed the blindfold. We were at our favorite mountain lodge! I thought, *Wow, I can really get into this!* And I did. I raced up the stairs with our luggage. And then—I pulled a muscle in my back! We spent the weekend in bed, all right. But it wasn't the romantic interlude either of us had in mind!"

When you think of a weekend getaway, what do you picture? One mom told us, "My picture is blank, because it will never happen! I've tried to get Fred to go off for a weekend but he won't budge. He says, 'Our marriage is fine; besides, we should be home with our children.'"

Recently, one father of three told us, "Wild horses wouldn't get Ethel to leave the kids for a weekend. I know better than to try!"

Maybe you relate to these two couples. You'd like a marriage booster but you know it will be nothing but a hassle. You'd like to infuse your relationship with fun, romance, and intimacy, but you're not sure how to pull it off. Well, be encouraged. Janie did it and so can you. Here's her side of the story:

"John had been under a lot of pressure at work. We kept talking about getting off for a weekend, but it just wasn't happening. I decided to take the initiative. The hardest part was finding baby-sitters for our two children. Our budget was tight so I arranged for Joy and Josh to stay with their cousins."

"John's boss was fascinated with what I was doing so he arranged for John to get off early on that Friday. I baked John's favorite treat—chocolate-chip cookies—and packed the car. I threw in the blindfold at the last minute. I could tell he was surprised and excited, but when he leaped out of the car and raced up the steps, I should have seen it coming. He literally couldn't move all weekend. But despite his bad back, we had many intimate conversations. Actually, I think we talked more that weekend away than any time since we've been married. But next time, I'm getting us a room on the first floor!"

Our advice: Start planning a getaway today. You can plan it together, or if your mate likes surprises, try Janie's approach. If you're still wondering if it's worth the effort to plan marriage getaways, read on.

Why You Need a Getaway

It takes work to build a marriage. A wedding is not a marriage, yet so much emphasis is put on the wedding itself. In 1993 alone, the American public spent thirty-two billion dollars on bridal products.* The wedding is just the threshold for a marriage. But from that moment on, we measure life in terms of before and after. Unfortunately, statistics show that there is

less than half a chance a marriage will go the
distance. And of those that do, many are not thriving and
growing.

Add children and the responsibilities of parenting them, and
the task of building a healthy marriage becomes increasingly
difficult. Focused times away give you a chance to regroup, re-
ignite romance, and deepen your marital bonds. We're convinced that getaways aren't just for fun, they're critical and necessary. So, if your marriage could do with a little stirring up, if
you're willing to take the risk, and if you really want to slow
down enough to create your own environment for growth and
change, plan your own getaway for two.

Just go easy on the stairs!

P. S. For Fred and Ethel, and for other parents who would
like to get away, we'll tell you how to leave the kids in the next
chapter!

*Bride's & Your New Home: Mattel; *Newsweek*, 2/7/94.

Chapter 44

No "Buts" About It

There's a three-letter word that is out to wreck your marriage. It's an instant marriage-enrichment stopper, and we're committed to helping you stomp it out! We've all heard it, and from time-to-time we've all said it. But if you say it too often, it's detrimental to your marital health. What is it? It's that little three-letter word, "But!"

"But" tends to pop out of our mouths when we're caught between our role as parents and our role as partners. Parenting responsibilities can be so demanding and overwhelming that we have little resistance to overcome the "buts." But if you're going to build your marriage while you parent your kids, you need some time away from those blessings of your family planning. You need to get away.

To help you do that, we're providing you with ammunition to beat the "buts" that might short-circuit your getaway.

"But our budget is too tight, how can we get away?"
- Borrow someone else's home or condo.
- Clip coupons. You may find some great motel or hotel deals like half-price, or two nights for one, or a package deal that includes meals.
- Take your own food and snacks with you.
- Open a special "getaway account." Save throughout the year.

• Instead of gifts for birthdays and special occasions, give your mate a coupon for a getaway.
• Go camping—not our choice, but we know some couples think it's the greatest!

"But our children are too young, how can we possibly leave them alone for two whole days?" (Fill in the ages and stages of your own children.)
• Remember you are doing it for their own good! You'll be a better parent if you get a break and you'll be a good model for your older children. Today, too many marriage models are shaky!
• Kids are survivors and will do just fine without you for a couple of days.
• They'll be there when you get back!
• The break will be good for both you and your children.
• Other competent caregivers can love and care for your children.

"But we don't have anyone to keep our children."
• Swap children with friends and then reciprocate and keep their children so they, too, can have a getaway. With three active boys, sometimes we had to divide and conquer. At times we actually kept two families' children on two different weekends in order to farm out our kids for one weekend. It was complicated, but it was worth it!
• Start a childcare cooperative with a few other families and reserve your time for weekends away.
• Save, save, and save, and hire a sitter for the weekend.
• Recruit willing relatives. If you have no relatives nearby, adopt grandparents, aunts, and uncles.

- Check with local Christian ministries. They may have single staff members who would love to be in a home for a weekend and would willingly take care of your children.
- If you have a Christian college in your area, you might find students who need extra spending money and would love to stay with your children.

"But you don't know our schedule. There is no time for a weekend getaway."
- If you can't pull off being away for the whole weekend, start with a twenty-four-hour getaway.
- Block out time now on next year's calendar.
- Think about why you want to do this. It is an investment in your marriage.
- List your priorities and act upon them! Your marriage should be near the top!

"But my spouse doesn't want to go. How can I convince him or her?"
- Offer to do all the planning and take care of all the details of getting away. Sometimes the reluctant mate is too stressed or tired and doesn't want the hassle of helping to pull it off.
- Plan your getaway around something you know your spouse enjoys—such as golfing, hiking in the mountains, or attending a sports or cultural event.
- If your mate likes surprises, kidnap him or her.
- Ask for a getaway for your birthday or for your anniversary.
- Recreate a special memory. Go back to where you spent your honeymoon.

"But we're just too tired to bother."

- Rent a motel or hotel room in your town. Spend the day together. Take naps and brainstorm how you can get off overnight in the future.
- Plan a getaway close to home. You don't have to go hours away for a retreat.
- Keep it simple. Eat out, and plan to sleep the first day! Remember you are not angels and you need sleep and rest!
- Plan ahead. Look for the season of the year when your workload is lighter. If you are in a retail business, for example, don't plan a getaway for December.
- Look for spur-of-the-moment opportunities when your children are spending the night with friends, visiting grandparents, or are otherwise engaged.
- If you are really too tired, trust us, you need this! Just do it!

Chapter 45

The Marriage Tree

Building a house is not without risks! If you've ever built a home or remodeled one, you know what we're talking about. At every turn are decisions waiting to be made. And even if you and your spouse generally agree on most things, you still probably have your little differences. Building a house together can expose them in a flash! You're not alone.

Our friends and mentors, Drs. David and Vera Mace, had their own story. Recently, we were visiting with Vera (David passed away several years ago). We decided to drive up and visit the house they built in the North Carolina mountains. After we arrived, we quickly congregated in our favorite part of the house—the screened porch. It was there that Vera told us this story.

When they were building their home, Vera very much wanted to build a screened porch. The major obstacle was a huge tree that was right where the screened porch was to be built. David loved the tree and didn't want to cut it down; Vera wanted the porch more than the tree. They just couldn't agree! There was no way to compromise and build around the tree, so finally David decided to give the tree to Vera as a love gift.

With a tinge of sadness, he watched the tree being cut down. Once it was down, the cutters pointed out that the tree was rotten on the inside and would have died, anyway. On that day,

David was glad he chose to defer to Vera's wishes.

For a marriage to go the distance, there are times when we all have to give up our wishes and go along with our mate's. If we always insist on getting our way, it's like we're living with a forest of rotten trees. Before we know it, they will come crashing down on us.

So how can you settle your differences in a loving, constructive way? The Maces helped us learn to do it with the three "Cs": *compromise, coexist*, and *capitulate*.

Compromise

This simply means that you each "give a little" to find a solution you both can live with. For example, when we built our house, Claudia didn't want a television in the living room. Dave did. Our solution was to put a small television in a wall cabinet where it is hidden, except on the rare occasions we actually use it.

Coexist

There are other times when we simply agree to disagree. After all, if we agreed on everything, only one of us would be necessary! The Maces call this kind of conflict resolution *coexistence*. Take food preferences, for example. Dave likes beets, but Claudia thinks they stink! So imagine Dave's surprise when one summer Claudia took him on a tour of her vegetable garden and showed him the beets, which she was growing just for him. Later, though, she confessed that she thought she had planted radishes.

Maybe you have differing political views or musical tastes. Some differences add spice to our marriage. But what do you do

when a decision has to be made, and as with
the Maces' screened porch, you simply can't agree?

Capitulate

One of you does what David Mace did with the tree and
porch. This "C" is called *capitulation*. He gave Vera a true gift of
love, for this was an important issue to both of them. But many
times couples argue over issues that just aren't that important,
or they are more important to one person than to the other.
Often, the simplest way to resolve the conflict is for the spouse
who doesn't have as much at stake to go along with the other.

When we were choosing colors for the walls in our home,
Dave questioned Claudia's choices. He just couldn't visualize
how it would look. Claudia could. Her feelings were much
stronger than Dave's, so he capitulated. In the end we both loved
the results.

Our caution is this: In a healthy marriage, there are differences and there is balance. Each partner should be willing to
give a gift of love to the other from time to time. There are
times to compromise, and there are times to agree to disagree.
You know that you have a problem, though, when one person
does all the giving and the other does all the taking.

Take it from us and the Maces, that's a rotten tree we can all
chop down!

Chapter 46

Seize the Day

Each year we look forward to our church's mission conference, and especially to meeting and talking to young families who are ministering in foreign countries. At one conference, we were drawn to Carlos and Genie, who lived and served in Mexico with their two young daughters.

We were able to share some of our parenting resources with them for their ministry in Mexico, and we also threw in a copy of our book, *The Marriage Track*. They were fascinated with the concept of "Marriage Supper Clubs" and said they wanted to try one when they returned to their mission field. We were pleased at their positive response.

So you can imagine our utter shock the next November when we received a letter from Carlos saying that Genie had died suddenly of meningitis. Now, his whole life was turned upside down—he was alone and had two young daughters to raise on his own.

As our church's mission conference rolled around, we wondered if Carlos would participate. He came, and we will never forget his conversation with us. He told us how he and Genie had gone back to Mexico and started their own marriage growth group. Since baby-sitters were at a premium, the couples took turns keeping each others' children between their small-group marriage get-togethers so each could have time alone together to apply what they were learning.

Five days before Genie died, the group had met, and the Sunday before she died, the other couple had kept Carlos and Genie's children and they had their last date. They had walked and talked and had a wonderfully leisurely just-for-two time—totally unaware it would be their last. Several days later, Genie became critically ill and suddenly died.

"Tell other couples," Carlos told us with his voice breaking, "not to take each other for granted, to seize the day, to take time for their marriages now. You just don't know how long you will have with each other."

Our hearts break every time we think of Carlos and the premature end of his marriage partnership with Genie. But we are thankful that they didn't put their marriage on the back burner until their kids grew up, that they seized the day while they could.

What about you? Are you taking advantage of today to build your marriage relationship? Too often, even in a healthy marriage, we let other things crowd out our commitment with one another and simply give our spouse the day's leftovers.

If you discovered you only had one day to be with your partner, how would you spend it? If you only had five minutes to talk, what would you tell your mate? It's so easy to take each other for granted and assume our spouses will always be there. We go through our busy days leaving too many things unsaid.

Why not take a few minutes alone to reflect on what you would really like to say to your mate? You might think about his or her character qualities, skills, or talents. Or think about the special things your mate does for you. What about his or her stability or abiding faith in God?

You could jot these things down and then use your own

creativity. Write a letter, write a poem, or compose a song. Or keep your list and give your mate one honest compliment each day for the next few weeks. It may become a mental habit even after your written list is gone.

Maybe today is the day to take your friend up on the offer to baby-sit, or for you and your spouse to plan that vacation for two you've been talking about for years. Whatever you choose to do, take Carlos' advice and "Seize the day!"

Heaven forbid, but it could be all that you have!

Chapter 47

Appreciating the In-laws

Most people don't think about it, but when they marry their Prince or Princess Charming, they also get the king, the queen, and the whole court! Despite all the "in-law/out-law" jokes, in-laws can play a significant role in how your marriage goes—and grows.

Healthy in-law relationships are a wonderful blessing in any marriage. Unhealthy in-law relationships can be a continual drain. What can you do to build healthy relationships with your in-laws?

The more mutual respect and enjoyment you experience with your in-laws, the more security and stability you and your spouse will feel in your marriage. We are in that stage of life where we have in-laws on both sides of us. We're the double-decker sandwich generation, and sometimes we need to affirm who we are and our own life priorities. Then we're able to deal positively with the extended family. Here are some of the things we are learning:

- We're not in the same season of life as our in-laws, so we need to try to understand their goals and what life is like from their perspective. The phrases, "When I was your age" or "You just don't understand our generation" do not work. The world is different for every generation and we need to respect that fact. Instead of lecturing when you see your in-laws overwhelmed with life, look for a practical way to lighten the load.

- Find the comfort zone between intimacy and distance. When we asked "What is your best advice for one who wants to be a great in-law?" we received the same answer in four different countries! Two simple words—"Stay away!" This wasn't the answer we expected, but it gave us a clue to one big dilemma in in-law relationships. How do you find the comfort zone between intimacy and distance?

Picture a seesaw with intimacy on one end and distance on the other. What you want to do is find the appropriate balance in your relationship. It's a continual balancing act, and it's easy to get off balance. The many changes in life create the need to adjust that balance. Some families enjoy getting together each Sunday for dinner, while others say, "Isn't it great that we get to see our married kids (or parents) several times a year?"

There are so many factors: where you live, children, jobs, financial resources. This is one area where you simply have to find what works for you. The more in-laws you add, the more complicated relationships become. You can't be as intimate with everyone as you are with your own spouse and children.

- Plan realistically for family visits. Encourage in-laws to visit, but also know your limits. When we visit our sons and their families, we try to time our visits so we leave before our welcome runs out. Sometimes we stay in a nearby motel instead of in their home if we think they need their space. Claudia's parents used to do this and it takes some pressure off the host family and doesn't inter- rupt family life. It works especially well when the visit is an extended one.
- Keep in touch through letters, videos, e-mail, and phone calls. Grandparents love getting artwork from grandchil-

dren, newspaper clippings about special awards, and pictures, of course. If the grandparents have an answering machine, let your children call at times when they are not home and leave personal messages. It works both ways. When our grandson, Walker, was born, Claudia left a personal message from "Oma" to Sophie, telling her how lucky Walker is to have a big sister like Sophie, and how much Oma loves her.

- Encourage grandparents to tell stories and read books on tape for your children. Another way to stay in touch is to make a little photo book of grandparents, cousins, aunts, and uncles—you can even use little sandwich bags. Put snapshots in the bags and then tie them together with yarn, making a special photo book for your child that is practically indestructible. And the best part is that it is all theirs!

- Share the lighter side of life. Learn to laugh and not take yourself so seriously! Grandparents love to hear funny little stories and sayings—like the time Billy, dressed in his Superman costume, thought he could fly and jumped out of the tree and skinned his knee. Or when Sally announced to the whole family, "I can tie my shoes, dress myself, and count to ten, so I must be grown up now."

- With in-laws, learn to accept love where you find it. Not all grandparents are "grandchildren friendly." Not all in-laws look for ways to encourage you in your marriage—like offering to baby-sit. Not all relatives are sensitive to others' needs. So give up expectations and accept love in whatever form it is offered. When the phone rings, whether it's that long-awaited call offering to keep your kids for the weekend or a call telling you they've booked a cruise for themselves, accept the loving help with your kids or be thankful that your parents are still together and love each other enough to plan a cruise.

To really appreciate in-laws, expect nothing and accept love where you find it! Oh yes, one other tip: start your own list now of how you would like to relate to your children as adults—and to your grandchildren! And don't forget that occasional cruise for just the two of you!

Chapter 48

First-Century Marriage Enrichment

We hear a lot about first-century Christians and their vibrant, living faith in Christ. But we seldom hear about what first-century marriages were like. You might have heard some sermons about gender roles or the status of women in the first century, but that's not what we're talking about, either. (However, we would note how highly Jesus esteemed women and that wherever the Christian message has gone in our world, the status of women has been raised.)

What we are talking about is the marriage relationship that transcends the culture (just as the faith of first-century Christians does), and stands as a noble example for Christian marriages today. Consider this description of Christian marriage as described by Tertullian in the second century:

> How beautiful is the marriage of two Christians, two who are one in hope, one in desire, one in the way of life they follow, one in the religion they practice. Nothing divides them, either in flesh or in spirit. They pray together, instructing one another, encouraging one another, strengthening one another. . . . They have no secrets from one another; they never shun each other's company; they never bring sorrow to each other's heart. They visit the sick and assist the needy. Psalms and hymns they sing to one another. . . . Hearing and seeing this, Christ rejoices. To such as these He gives His

peace. Where there are two together, there also He is present.*

Does this quote describe your marriage relationship? If it does, you have a growing and loving marriage. If you haven't quite found this kind of marital harmony, you can use this description as a model for building a Christian marriage today. Some excellent marriage enrichment principles from this 1,800-year-old quote will still work for us today.

How beautiful is the marriage of two Christians, two who are one in hope, one in desire, one in the way of life they follow, one in the religion they practice. . . . Nothing divides them, either in flesh or in spirit.

First Principle: In a first-century Christian marriage, both were Christians. That's basic. Not Christian in name only or just belonging to the same church, but living faith permeating their existence together. They were one in hope and desire and it affected the way they lived!

Today, many people claim to have Christian marriages. Yet the divorce rate among Christians is indistinguishable from the general population. If Christians followed the first-century model, and allowed "nothing to divide them, either in flesh or in spirit," wouldn't that statistic be different?

Application: Renew your commitment to your spouse, and together renew your commitment to Jesus Christ. Let your faith in God be the foundation of your marriage.

They pray together, instructing one another, encouraging one another, strengthening one another.

Second Principle: First-century couples built each other's faith and, in turn, their marriage relationship. They were on the same team and concentrated on the positive aspects of their marriage. They were united and would never even think of the other as an enemy!

Application: Start the practice of having a daily couple time—time when you can pray together and focus on each other.

They have no secrets from one another; they never shun each other's company; they never bring sorrow to each other's heart.

Third Principle: They were transparent with each other. They spent time together and worked on their communication skills. They avoided attacking each other and were considerate of each other's feelings.

Application: Be willing to be transparent with your mate. Don't be afraid to express your inner feelings to each other, but in a way that is not attacking. Follow the example of Christ by putting your mate first and looking for ways to serve each other.

They visit the sick and assist the needy.

Fourth Principle: The couple described had a focus larger that just the two of them. Together they reached out and ministered to others. They found joy in serving others. They took care of their relationship, but they also transcended any "me first" attitudes.

Application: What can you do today to help someone less fortunate than you? Talk together about how you might develop a ministry together.

Psalms and hymns they sing to one another. . . . Hearing and seeing this, Christ rejoices. To such as these He gives His peace. Where there are two together, there also He is present.

Fifth Principle: First-century marriages were marked by a joyful spirit, surrounded by the peace of God and His presence. When life got tough and problems came, the people in this marriage knew that God was in control of their lives and their marriage. They knew they could trust in Him.

Application: Focus on things above. Know that God is in control. Remind each other of God's goodness and encourage each other through psalms and hymns.

When you work to keep your marriage Christ-centered, God will give you His peace that passes all understanding! Then you, too, will have an enriched, growing first-century Christian marriage!

*From David and Vera Mace, *What's Happening to Clergy Marriages?* (Nashville: Abingdon Press, 1980), 97.

Chapter 49

Rekindling Romance

Would you like to infuse your marriage with fun, romance, and intimacy? You may be thinking that it's easier said than done. If so, you're right, but fun, romance, and intimacy are important ingredients for growing a healthy marriage. Hugs, kisses, secret signals, silly notes in each other's lunch, little gifts for no reason—all of these little things add up to help you affirm your love and commitment to each other.

"What will our kids think?" asked Alice. "If they see us acting all silly and lovey-dovey, they'll think we're crazy!"

We were happy to tell Alice that romance in the home is a family booster as well as a marriage booster. So many children today live in fear that their parents will get divorced. Statistics verify their fears. So when you romance your mate, you're actually doing your children a favor—no matter how much they tease or roll their eyes!

Romance is not something reserved for the bedroom. Being thoughtful and kind to each other will spill over into your lovemaking. Romance is more of an attitude that is caught. Here are some tips to help it be contagious at your house:

- Be affectionate. Affection can be habit forming. Once, after we spoke at a sweethearts banquet in a church, an elderly couple shyly told us one of the ways they show affection. "When we were first married, someone suggested we shower together," the petite woman said. "We tried it, and it was so much fun, we've been showering together every morning since!" Her husband added, "After all the years, it's still fun to wash each other's hair and back."

The shower is a great place to be affectionate. Make a list of other places and ways you can show affection. Phone calls, e-mail messages, cooking your mate's favorite dish, holding hands, giving a peck on the cheek—all of these small displays of affection add romance to your relationship.

- Be a listener. A Kansas newspaper once ran an advertisement that said, "Without making any comments, I will listen to you talk for thirty minutes. Just $5." Would you believe that ten to twenty people called that number every day from all over the United States?

Yet, in the hectic pace of family life, it's easy to tune the other out and not really listen. We all need someone who will listen to us—and in marriage, that someone is your mate. One of the most important lovemaking skills you can learn is to communicate while you are loving each other. This includes listening with your heart as well as your ears. Make an effort to listen to your mate, as well as to share your own feelings. We guarantee it will be a romance enhancer.

- Be adventurous. Look for ways to be bold and spontaneous. You're limited only by your imagination. Call in late for work and grab a couple of hours with each other after the kids go to school. Plan a middle-of-the-day rendezvous. Ralph and Lisa work near each other, and from time to time they coordinate their breaks to meet in the car in the parking lot. It's one creative way they grab a few minutes together to just talk and hold hands.
- Take your time. We are so used to rushing through our days that when we do make time for romance, we forget to

reduce our speed! We're in such a
hurry, we miss a great deal of the enjoyment derived
from just getting there.

Remember that whatever you do to promote romance, getting there is half the fun. Go for a walk and hold hands. Stop
along the way for a kiss or two. By taking the time to cuddle, to
laugh, and to share intimate thoughts, you will enhance the
romance between you.

- Be thankful to God. Remember that love and romance in
  marriage is a unique gift from God. He designed our souls
  to tenderly touch each other and our bodies with the
  capacity for pleasure. So relax and enjoy each other with
  God's blessings.
- Plan time for two when you can focus on each other. And
  don't underestimate the importance of dates and getaways!
- Learn to laugh. When stress hits and your romantic times
  don't work out as planned, keep your sense of humor.
  Learning to laugh and have fun together will enhance
  romance in your marriage.

You can rekindle the romance in your relationship. We love
what the Spanish poet Antonio Machado said:

"I thought the fire was out in my fireplace,

I stirred the ashes, And I burned my hands."

Go ahead and fan the flames of romance in your marriage.
With love, patience, persistence, and good humor, you'll find
romance is alive and well in your home.

Chapter 50

The Marriage Journey

Leading marriage seminars helps us build our own marriage, but sometimes we stop and realize that marriage is a journey—we will never arrive! There's always room for growth.

Years ago when we lived in Vienna, we led our marriage workshops for small groups in our home. Naturally, our three sons would wander in and out and at times sit and listen to what we had to say. One statement we still emphasize in our workshop is, "Communication is the breath of life in any marriage."

Did you ever notice how children are like computers? They store up your words to use at the appropriate time!

When we lived in Vienna, every year right before Christmas, we went off for a few days with several other families for a short ski vacation. It was a tradition we all looked forward to.

One year, we were headed to a new location. Dave asked Claudia to call our friend Betty to get directions. When Claudia called Betty, she responded, "Let me get Rob on the phone; he knows right where it is."

Claudia answered, "Dave is the one who needs them, so I'll get him on the phone and he and Rob can talk."

Fast-forward to the next week. Excited about our ski vacation, we were all packed into our station wagon, heading up a narrow alpine road. It was snowing and the roads were icy. Things were already a little tense when we came to a fork in the road.

"Which way do we go?" Dave asked.

"What do you mean, which way, didn't Rob give you directions?"

"Directions?"

Dave and Rob had talked on the phone, but neither knew the purpose of their conversation was to get directions.

It was cold and snowing outside, but things were definitely heating up in our car. Then our oldest son said, "Ah, yes, communication is the breath of life in any marriage!" That day we desperately needed a breath of fresh air!

Have you ever found yourself in a similar situation? You think you have it down. Your marriage is great. You know how to communicate. You've got a game plan. But then you come to a fork in the road of life. And it's then you realize that marriage is more complicated than you thought!

It's times like these that help us to remember that marriage is a journey, not a destination. We will never arrive. Our marriage will move forward or backward, but it won't stand still. It's a fluid relationship. And the moment we stop working on it is the moment it will stop being vital and living! So what can we do to keep our marriage growing?

By the way, we did take the right fork on that mountain road, and we arrived at our destination safely. Sometimes we're lucky and things works out. But it's always better to know which way to go before you come to the crossroads.

So as we come to the close of this book, we'd like to leave you with several routes you can take to keep your marriage on track and moving along:

1. Consider participating in a formal Marriage Enrichment Weekend. There are a number of excellent programs available. We suggest that you look for one that is led by a

couple for other couples. You also want one that is interactive—giving you and your mate time to talk to each other. We've found as we have worked with couples over the years, successful marriages come not so much from knowing what to do as from doing what we know. Small groups may also offer you more focused help. (See Appendix I for suggested programs.)

2. Start your own marriage-enrichment library. Begin to collect books on marriage enrichment, especially those that give practical exercises you can use to build your marriage. Consider including videos and periodicals in your library.

3. Form your own marriage growth group. You could even use the chapters in this book to kick off the discussion.

4. Start your own daily sharing time. Ten minutes over a cup of coffee or tea will give you the opportunity to touch emotionally and connect for the day.

5. Of course, don't forget to date your mate!

Take it from us, make the time to build your marriage. Your children will wait while you take time for your marriage, but your marriage won't wait until your kids grow up. Now is the time to ignite the flame of love! Be willing to do what it takes to keep love alive—to build your marriage. Then you will be able to pass on a legacy of love to the next generation!

Appendix I

Resources

Consider a marriage enrichment experience such as:

- Marriage Alive Seminar. David and Claudia Arp will help you renew and energize your marriage with fun, intimacy, and romance. For information about how your church can host this six-hour workshop, or to schedule the Arps to speak, contact:

  > Alive Communications, 1465 Kelly Johnson Blvd., Suite 320, Colorado Springs, CO 80920.
  > Phone: (719) 260-7080; Fax:(719) 260-8223

- Marriage Enrichment Weekend. The Association of couples in Marriage Enrichment (ACME), founded by David and Vera Mace, is a network of couples working for better marriages. For information about upcoming weekends, call 1-800-634-8325.

- Marriage Encounter. A Christian ministry founded by Father Calvo in Spain, Marriage Encounter offers weekend retreats to help couples grow closer to each other, and to God. United Marriage Encounter is an interdenominational Christian expression of the Marriage Encounter Weekend. For information about upcoming weekends, call 1-800-334-8920.

Book and Video Resources

- Dave and Claudia Arp, *The Second Half of Marriage: Facing the Eight Challenges of Every Long-Term Marriage* (Grand Rapids: Zondervan, 1996).

- Dave and Claudia Arp, *The Ultimate Marriage Builder: A Do-it-Yourself Encounter Weekend for You and Your Mate* (Nashville: Thomas Nelson, 1994).
- Dave and Claudia Arp, *52 Dates for You and Your Mate* (Nashville: Thomas Nelson, 1993).
- Dave and Claudia Arp, *The Love Book* (Nashville: Thomas Nelson, 1994).
- Dave and Claudia Arp, *60 One-Minute Family Builder Series* (Nashville: Thomas Nelson, 1993).
- Claudia Arp and Linda Dillow, *The Big Book of Family Fun* (Nashville: Thomas Nelson, 1994).
- PEP Groups. Parents Encouraging Parents. Video-based small group parenting resources for the local church, including:

  PEP Groups for Parents of Teens. A very versatile program to help parents get ready for and survive the adolescent years. The emphasis is on devising a game plan to release your teens into adulthood while building a positive relationship that will last a lifetime (David C. Cook, Colorado Springs, 1994).

  PEP Groups for MOMs. Provides mothers with supportive friendships and helps them build positive relationships with their children (David C. Cook, Colorado Springs, 1994).

For more information about any of the Arps' resources contact: Marriage Alive International, Inc. P.O. Box 30148, Knoxville, TN 37930
Phone: (423) 691-8505

Magazines We Recommend

- *Christian Parenting Today.* A dynamic publication designed to help you experience the joys and meet the challenges of raising your children to be all they can be—spiritually, emotionally, socially and physically. Published six times per year. For subscription information, please call 1-800-238-2221, or write to *Christian Parenting Today*, P.O. Box 545, Mt. Morris, IL 61054.

- *Virtue.* An honest, passionate, insightful celebration of the contemporary Christian woman and her relationship with God, her spouse, family, and friends. Published six times per year by Good Family Magazines. For subscription information, please call 1-800-238-2221, or write to *Virtue*, P. O. Box 456, Mt. Morris, IL 61054.

- *Parents of Teenagers.* From cover to cover, you will be encouraged with biblically-sound expert advice, helping you to grasp the complexities of your teen's world and giving you the tools to build a strong, lasting relationship. Published ten times per year by Good Family Magazines. For subscription information, please call 1-800-238-2221, or write to *Parents of Teenagers*, P. O. Box 482, Mt. Morris, IL 1054.

- *Marriage Partnership.* Published quarterly by Christianity Today, Inc., is an excellent resource for enriching your marriage. Each issue contains several marriage builders that are fun, positive, and easy to use. For subscription information please call 1-800-627-4942, or write to *Marriage Partnership*, P. O. Box 37060, Boone, IA 50037-0060.

Appendix II

Dedication

You might consider using or adapting this dedication if you move into a new home. Or, you might want to rededicate your present home to the Lord and His service.

Dedication of the Home of David and Claudia Arp

Leader: Unless the Lord builds the house, its builder labors in vain.

People: May the Lord bless you from Zion all the days of your life; may you live to see your children's children.

Leader: Throughout human history, God has called men and women together in marriage, and has moved them to build houses in which their love for Him, for one another, for family, and neighbors will take such concrete expression that the building will become a home, an outpost of God's kingdom.
With gratitude to God for Dave and Claudia, and for this house in which they will love and labor together, we are gathered here to dedicate this building to our merciful God, and to ask His blessing upon it, to place His Son's name upon it, and to pray for His Spirit to fill it.

Let us pray. Almighty and most merciful God, our heavenly Father, thank You for making us in Your image to share in the ordering of Your world. Thank You that, although we are sojourners on Earth, we are not wanderers. Bless this house and all who live herein. Fill each one afresh with Your Spirit; mark this place with the name of Your Son, our Lord and Savior Jesus Christ, in whose most holy name we pray. Amen.

(At the home's entrance.)

Leader: Let the door be opened. Peace be to this house, and to all who enter here. In the name of the Father, and of the Son, and of the Holy Spirit.

People: Amen.

(In the entrance hall.)

Leader: Our help is in the name of the Lord;

People: The Maker of heaven and earth.

Leader: Let us pray.

Together: Everliving Father, watchful and caring, our source and our end, all that we are and all that we have is Yours. Accept us now in Christ, as we dedicate this place to You. May it be a place of grace and forgiveness, of love and compassion, of creativity and joy. Be always present to illumine and bless Your people. Amen.

(In the living room.)

Leader: Father, may Dave and Claudia within this room have eyes and ears open to You, to one another, and to those who will come to share their lives, enjoy their company, and seek their wisdom. May they rejoice with those who rejoice and weep with those who weep. And in the quiet hours before the fire, may they always know the pleasure of Your presence.

People: Now fill this room with Your presence, Lord, we pray. Amen.

(In the kitchen.)

Leader: Creator of all, You have given us good things to eat from the field and from the flock. You have blessed our table fellowship with Your presence. So may the meals prepared and eaten in this place be in the truest sense sacramental meals that manifest Your presence and Your grace.

People: Now fill this room with Your presence, Lord, we pray. Amen.

(In the master bedroom.)

Leader: Lord Christ, You have pursued us as a lover, and have conquered us with Your Spirit. Father God, You have shown us a mother's love in creating and recreating us, in carrying us, sustaining us, and staying with us to the end. In this room, may Dave and Claudia experience something of those aspects of Your love, as they celebrate their love, and find rest and renewal in sleep.

People: Now fill this room with Your presence, Lord, we pray. Amen.

(Other rooms. People scatter and pray for the house, then regather in the living room.)

Leader: Now, Father, Son and Holy Spirit, sanctify this house;
People: For everything in heaven and on earth is Yours.
Leader: Yours, Lord, is the kingdom;
People: And You are exalted as head over all. Amen.*

*Written for the Arps' house blessing by the Reverend John Wood, pastor of Cedar Springs Presbyterian Church, Knoxville, Tennessee.